In October and December 2008, groups of Year 10 pupils from four Lincolnshire schools met together at Bishop Grosseteste University College. There, they listened to a first-hand account of escaping from the Iranian army and a lecture on the history of biography. They also heard Kate Clanchy, award-winning poet, journalist and playwright, talking about her latest book, *What Is She Doing Here?* This concerns the five years she spent living closely with Antigona, a Kosovan refugee, and Kate was able to talk in detail about the many complex ethical and literary issues involved in writing such a sensitive biography.

Between the October and December meetings, the Year 10s each interviewed a person who lived in Lincolnshire but had been born abroad. Their task was then to write the stories of these new arrivals. The extent to which they decided to tell their own story was left up to them. The resulting pieces are gathered here. I hope you enjoy reading this book and that you learn from it about the people around you, and perhaps also about yourself.

I would like to thank the pupils and teachers of Kesteven and Grantham Girls' School, Grantham; North Kesteven School, North Hykeham; The Priory Academy LSST, Lincoln and William Farr CE Comprehensive School, Welton for the hard work, patience and commitment that they have shown to this project. I would also like to acknowledge the co-operation of the pupils in other schools who were interviewed for this project and the time and effort put in by their teachers to ensure that all the various issues surrounding publication were eventually overcome.

For a free teachers' guide to using this book in the classroom please email: swillshaw@cfbt.com

Steve Willshaw
Senior School Improvement Consultant

Contents

Zemar's story

Whilst standing by the side of the dusty road, Zemar heard a distant noise, sounding like a faraway plane coming closer. It was a lorry! It was his chance. He knew that he had to take it then or he never would. Trembling with nerves and excitement, he struggled up into the back of the lorry. There were already a few people inside, mostly around Zemar's age. They exchanged smiles of acceptance and understanding, and the lorry driver carried on his journey. All Zemar knew was that he was going to England. He had heard from books that it was a beautiful, modern place. He thought that anything would be better than Afghanistan. The dust from the road twisted up as if it was a hurricane as the lorry steadily trundled on. That was something he wasn't going to miss. There was no hurry.

As the journey was entering its seventh week, even though to Zemar it felt like seven months, he realised that they were nearing their destination. His nerves began to take him over, which was understandable given that he was only 15 at the time. He started to ask himself questions: What if he hated it? What if he couldn't find a job? What if he got sent back? What if...? As the unbearable journey came to an end, Zemar's nerves soon turned into excitement at the prospect of a new, better life in this foreign country.

Looking back, Zemar thought about how excruciatingly difficult a decision it was for him to make, a choice between staying in Afghanistan with the family he loved so much, and going to England where he would have a better lifestyle. Zemar's mother of course did everything she could to stop him going; however, his father eventually persuaded her that it was Zemar's decision. Zemar didn't want his life to be as tedious as his father's, farming all day long and for what? More farming the next day. No doubt it would be the same for Zemar's eight-year-old brother, Namir.

Finally, after what seemed to him like years, Zemar found himself on the ferry. After the cramped, smelly boat journey the lorry started to move. They had arrived! Zemar suddenly felt a rush of adrenalin as he breathed in the fresh air and realised his life was going to change for the better. Zemar did have a distant cousin living somewhere in the south of England; however, he didn't have the faintest idea where to go. He was going to have to make it on his own. Zemar found the tall buildings and the busyness of this strange country extremely daunting; it was the complete opposite of all that he was used to in Afghanistan. It was to be the beginning of a new life.

Hannah Walker

Ramadan

Namir and her seven siblings walked, hand in hand, back to the family house, their backs aglow with the last of the day's sunlight. Today was the last day of Ramadan, the last day of fasting before Eid-ul-Fitr. Namir should really have felt some sense of achievement, but she only felt hungry, tired and rather sullen. Despite her disgruntled mood, when she arrived home Namir faked a smile and went about her daily chores without any complaint.

As soon as the sun sank below the horizon, Namir, her mother and her siblings sat down at the table, ready to eat iftar (a light meal eaten after sunset, consisting mainly of dates). Together they prayed to Allah and ate in silence. That night Namir slept soundly, excited about the feast the following day.

The second she woke up, Namir sprang out of bed and stormed downstairs to the kitchen, where she found her mother busily cleaning the floor. She noticed her mother had a particularly large smile on her face and a certain spring in her step, something she had lost years ago, since her father left to go and work in England. Rather than ask, Namir decided to let her mother enjoy whatever was making her so jubilant.

An hour later Namir's mother began singing, not the type of dry religious songs they sang in the mosque, but a sweet romantic tune, and almost like the lullabies she used to sing to Namir and her siblings when they were younger.

Curiosity got the better of Namir.

'Mother, you are very happy today! Is this because our cousins are coming? Or because Ramadan is over and you didn't break your fasting?'

'It will all be unravelled in the end,' her mother replied merrily, and with that she walked swiftly away.

Namir's cousins arrived later that day, including her best friend Zalmai. Zalmai and she had grown up together and conquered whatever life threw at them. They didn't get to see each other very much any more, as Zalmai had to continue his education and Namir wasn't able to further hers. Due to the fact they were both a different sex, time spent together had to be limited. So today was a special day for them both.

As lunchtime approached, Namir found herself sitting on the cold floor, in a crowded room. The loud chitchat of her family filled her ears and the sweet scent of oranges filled her nose, whilst the hollow ache of hunger occupied her stomach and an odd anticipation her head. She was still thinking about what her mother had said to her earlier that day...

'I would like to make an announcement,' a voice interrupted Namir's thoughts. It was her mother. Was this what Namir had been waiting to hear all day?

'Zelgai, Ajani, Namir, Muni, Zemar, Uzuri, Yasir and Suzan,' she addressed them individually, 'I have some important news for you.'

'What is it, Ma?' Muni, the youngest, asked eagerly.

'Yes, do tell us, Mother,' Zemar, the oldest, added.

'Well...,' Namir's mother began, her grin widening. 'You have not seen your father for nine years, but now he has a new job, as a taxi driver and delivery man.'

'What does this mean, Ma?' Namir asked.

'Well...,' there was a long pause, 'it means we can go and live with him, in England. One big family again. Will that not be great?'

The rhetorical question was never answered and a few months later Namir found herself in a large school in Lincoln, talking to me.

Namir was 17 and lived in a four-roomed flat, with the other nine members of her family. She thought England was cold and the food here was bad, she liked her friends at school, but the other pupils could be a bit rough. She told me that the best thing about living here in England was that she felt safe.

In fact her exact words were 'In Afghanistan there is always shooting and in the morning you hear the bomb blasts.'

'Do you think you will ever return to live in Afghanistan?' I asked, shocked by her previous answer. I had only ever seen the awful state the world was in on the news; now it was becoming more of a reality.

'Yes, when I am president,' she smiled.

'You are a very ambitious person then,' I guessed.

'Now I am getting an education I can be president when I am older.' Before I could enquire any more. the bell rang for lunch and we had to say our goodbyes.

Compared to her life, my life sounds boring. I lived in Newcastle and moved 154 miles; she lived in Afghanistan and moved 3,554 miles, and yet we both ended up living in one small town called Lincoln. Sometimes it scares me how small the world is.

Eliza Eady

An Unexpected Encounter

As I walked down the halls of St. Matthew's School, I started to feel nauseous and intimidated by the task at hand. What would I ask them? Would I offend them? Would I be able to understand what they were saying? I wanted to feel excited about this opportunity, but the truth was I didn't. I just felt rather sick. Opening the door into the room where we were to interview the foreign pupils, I was the one who felt foreign. I felt very self-conscious, I felt like an outsider: like I was somebody who didn't belong. We were put together in pairs and I sat down next to a girl called Fareiba.

I introduced myself, and she did the same, and an awkward silence followed. 'I don't speak much English,' she said suddenly. 'If you don't understand please tell me.' I wondered why she didn't speak much English and I asked how long she had lived in Lincoln. 'Oh, only six months.' I was amazed, given my complete lack of ability to learn French for the past three years, that in six months she was able to speak and understand English so well. When I told her this, she blushed and said, 'I studied English when I lived in Afghanistan. Maybe that's helped me to learn the language.'

Fareiba lived in Afghanistan, in the city of Kabul with her mother, brother and four sisters. Her father emigrated to Lincoln when she was nine to bring in more money for the family. When I asked how she felt about this, she saw it as a necessity: 'I was sad when he left, but my mum said he was trying to get us a better life.' I asked what she meant by 'better life' and she told me more about how Kabul is a thriving city. However, it is surrounded by many conflicts: news of bombings and deaths are nothing out of the ordinary. What could I say to that?

A long awkward silence followed again, and then she said something I really wasn't expecting. 'Is there any fighting in England?' I looked at her as if she was stupid. Of course there's no fighting in England, my country is completely different to yours, and I replied with a blunt 'No'. However, a moment after,

I realised that actually there has been fighting in England not so long ago, involving the IRA and that, in fact, Fareiba and I were not quite so different as I believed we must be. I was so ashamed at how I saw her country in relation to mine that I couldn't even look at her.

It started me thinking, are we really that different? There were obvious differences such as our appearances. Her skin colour was quite dark whereas mine is very pale. Our age; she was 17 and I was 14 and our families; I have only one brother whereas she has five other siblings. I realised that I had been bombarding her with questions about her country, her culture and her opinions on England. I'd asked her neither about her hobbies nor something simple like what she likes to eat. I apologised to her about this and she said, 'Oh, don't worry it's fine,' and I began to ask her more questions, this time about things she liked to do.

'I love shopping! My favourite shop is Primark and I also like history books. What's the bookshop called again?'

'Waterstone's?'

'That's it!'

We both laugh, and for the first time since I sat down next to Fareiba I feel comfortable with her, and I think she feels comfortable with me. We continue talking about odds and ends and discover that we both like the same type of music. We almost have an argument about the different types of films we like, but the atmosphere is light and sociable.

The first half-hour seemed like a decade, with the awkward silences and the sensitive topics, but as soon as I realised that Fareiba was a person, not just an interviewee, time seemed to fly by. All too soon we were called to leave, and I said my goodbyes to Fareiba, knowing it was not likely we would see each other again.

As I left the room, I wasn't thinking about the hardships Fareiba had faced, or the differences in our lifestyles, or even the daunting idea of writing this essay. I was thinking about what a nice person I had just met, and walking back down the corridor I felt a sense of relief that the interview had gone so well. However, I still felt rather sick because it was one o'clock, I hadn't had lunch, and I was starving!

Lois Wildman

Yasir's story

We met on 4th December 2008. I stared at the 15-year-old boy. As the boy looked back at me, I gazed into his face. I saw nothing. He showed no emotion and his facial expression conveyed no sign of happiness, nor of sadness. This boy surely couldn't have had much of an eventful life. He showed no mental scarring. An emotional past would usually be splashed across a person's face, as noticeable as black paint slapped onto white paper. This boy had none of that. The boy sat rigid and still, probably trying to make himself appear as small as possible. This was strange considering he was probably the tallest and most muscular person in the room. I took a seat in front of him. He let out a quiet noise that was almost inaudible. I fidgeted in my seat. I didn't know if that noise was a laugh of happiness or an anxious whimper. Silence hung above us like a banging headache that just won't go away. I let out a big grin, hoping this would cover over my worries. The boy smiled uneasily back.

'Yasir,' he replied after I asked him what his name was. He was a quiet boy, which surprised me as I was expecting a booming voice to emanate from his large frame. This soft voice contrasted with mine as I was speaking relatively loudly, attempting to break the awkwardness between us. I asked him where he had lived before emigrating to England. He was an Afghan boy, having lived in Afghanistan for approximately 15 years with his parents and younger brother. He had led a simple but hard life in Afghanistan, he told me. He'd wake early every morning with no means of education, working to earn money and food for his family as a full-time farmer. He told me of how he'd sow seeds, morning and night, and of his father, Basheer, who'd collect the crops, hoping to satisfy the family's hunger. His mother, Tamana was a typical housewife, having to prepare the food, clean their tiny excuse for a house, and take care of six-year-old Sidiq who'd sometimes attempt to help Yasir with the sowing of the seeds, before becoming bored and falling asleep.

Yasir and his family were all extremely faithful Muslims, always visiting their local mosque four times a day, without fail, along with dozens of other local citizens. I knew how strongly Muslims believed in their Islamic religion and how loyal they were to their god Allah, so I didn't linger on the subject much, only vaguely mentioning a religious education lesson I had once been in.

I asked how he came to be in England.

Yasir looked at the field, exhausted from a whole day of sowing seeds. His desperate search for shade brought him to the trunk of the tree. He sat and leaned against it, gazing at the field. Oh, how often he would sit in that very place staring at that dreaded field. Oh, how much he wished he could stop this awful routine of sowing seeds. How much he wished he could give up his job of standing outside under the blazing sun every day. How much he wished he could have a proper education. Yasir wanted to make something of his life and he knew that couldn't be done in a country like Afghanistan.

Yasir must have dozed off. He awoke at what must have been 8.00 pm as the sun was beginning to set. A blurry figure was next to the house, waving and calling his name. Yasir recognised it to be his mother.

'Yasir! Where have you been all day?' Yasir rubbed his eyes, stood up slowly and brushed himself down. He walked towards the house as Tamana carried on shouting.

'Come on! Your uncle's here and he wants to talk to you!' Surprised, Yasir approached and entered the house.

'How would you like to come to England with me, Yasir?' Everyone apart from Sidiq was standing in the kitchen. Yasir raised his eyebrows at Uncle Abdul whilst he glanced at his parents who were nodding in agreement across the room.

'Oh yes, I think this is perfect for you, Yasir,' said Basheer.

'You've been lazy and unhappy recently… I think this may be the trick to get you going again!' Tamana said. This was perfect, just as Yasir's father had said. This was just what Yasir had been waiting for. His heart lifted as he imagined the new life he would have in England.

'Well, let's get going then! Are we all going to go on an aeroplane or something?' Yasir said.

His parents and uncle exchanged looks of uneasiness. Yasir looked at the three of them, confused.

'What?' Uncle Abdul looked down and scuffed his feet against the floor, apparently trying to sweep the dust away from him.

'Well the thing is Yasir… it's only you that can go. Tamana and Basheer are going to have to stay here with Sidiq. I'm sorry it has to be like this but…' Uncle Abdul paused mid-sentence, avoiding eye contact with Yasir.

'Only you would be able to get out of the country safely…' Abdul paused again and turned to look at Yasir, but found he was looking away towards the field, almost ignoring him. Millions of thoughts rushed through Yasir's head: go to England, without mother, father or Sidiq? What would I do in England all by myself? How would I cope? But England is such a highly developed country… I'd do anything just for a visit.

'And what you said about going in an aeroplane Yasir, that isn't exactly the case…' Yasir carried on, ignoring him, thoughts of Big Ben and the Houses of Parliament and beefeaters buzzed through his mind.

'I can only take you in a lorry,' Abdul finished. The word 'lorry' caught Yasir's attention and he turned to face Uncle Abdul's solemn face. This lorry was also news to his parents as they stared at Abdul with an expression of shock on their faces that Yasir couldn't bear to look at.

It wasn't the fact that he had travelled in a lorry all the way to England that surprised me, it was the matter-of-fact tone in his voice that caused me to stop writing and look sympathetically at the Afghan boy.

Yasir said yes. He was 15 years old. He wasn't a baby any more. He would cope fine in England. He would live in a nice house and earn lots of money and have servants and drink tea all the time. How bad could travelling in a lorry be?

The next week, after Yasir had packed all his belongings and said his goodbyes to his family, he climbed in the back of the lorry, forming a pile with some empty boxes in the corner.

'You all ready?' Uncle Abdul called to Yasir from the driver's seat. Yasir took one last look at his mother crying, his father waving, and his brother tugging at his mother's shirt, looking confused.

'What's happening? Why is Yasir in that lorry?' Sidiq asked loudly, but got no reply. Tamana was stuck for words.

'Don't forget to visit the local mosque where you're staying, Yasir!' Basheer shouted.

The realisation that he wouldn't see his family for years, maybe forever, jumped up at him. His mother and father would never see him fall in love or get married or have children. But what seemed the worst to him was that Sidiq would grow up scarcely able to remember that he once had a brother. Yasir's eyes burned, and he looked towards the front of the lorry.

'Ready when you are,' Yasir replied. The engine started, the tyres shook and the door to the lorry was closed tight, causing every source of light to drain away, leaving Yasir in total darkness.

And that journey could have lasted forever. Miles of road were travelled along as Yasir sat alone in the darkness that to him didn't appear so dark any more. He sat in the corner, with a few boxes, a blanket and a pillow for company. At first, Uncle Abdul had stopped regularly to let Yasir out for some fresh air, but that had all ceased now. He didn't want to risk Yasir being caught as an illegal immigrant. Home felt like a million miles away. He was being taken to a place he wasn't familiar with and a place that wasn't familiar with him. People would think him mad. He could have been mad. The darkness had become his friend and the lack of sunlight messed with Yasir's mind as he sat staring at the boxes that appeared to sprout faces which laughed evilly at him. His breathing became deep and the temperature inside the back of the dingy lorry gradually rose. He constantly shook along with the beat of the lorry moving, and remorse hung in Yasir's head as he travelled further away from home.

Mad thoughts of returning home to his family kept sneaking into his head. Even though he thought these ridiculous (it was much too late to go back now), a tiny part of him kept hoping that it might actually happen, that if he hoped more than anyone had ever hoped before, then maybe he just might get a second chance and his hopes would come true. But for now, as his clothes grew too large for his body and his body shrank, becoming too small for his clothes, he was left to turn insane and with the only thing that had stayed with him since the start of the ride. Those tears had accompanied him for the whole length of the journey.

Katie Rooke

Najwa's story

The warmth radiates not only from the blazing sun above, but through the crowded streets flourishing with life and laughter. This impression serves as a veil, shrouding the poverty. Within the marketplace, a girl stands. She finds comfort in the warm air and the familiarity of language that is accentuated within the density of the crowd around her. Silhouetted in the distance, the pyramids mark Cairo as her homeland. A wisp of wind whispers her name – Najwa, here you belong.

A sharp gust of cold bites at her fingertips, and she is again awoken by the dim reality she inhabits: England. The screaming of the other children returns to her in a crescendo; she is in a playground. Alone, she is the new girl. 'Foreigner' they call her, and the distance of her homeland is mirrored in the distance the children push her away. They mock her for the features that define her: her dark eyes, her dark eyebrows, her religion. This abuse continues, behind the dismissal that children will be children; they'll be laughing tomorrow at the person who next calls their teacher 'Mum'.

So, from a young age, Najwa's earthly paradise was taken away from her. Egypt became but a distant memory. For the sake of her father, they had moved in the hope of better job prospects. Her emptiness remained constant, however, and was only somewhat soothed by her mother's love. Love, it seemed, would aid her through the next difficult years, as a candle through her darkest nights. Her mother, the spiritual angel, would open her eyes to the opportunities the world could offer her as Allah once did to His followers. Though blinded by the restrictions enforced by her father, she retained the right of free will, until the separation of her parents.

From then on, Najwa vowed to work through each day as a new challenge, her motive being to amount to the success she would have otherwise achieved, had her father allowed her talents to emerge. The thought of Allah, and her dedication to

Him, prevailed, as the first dismal summers and yet more dreary winters slowly faded in and then out of the present. Like a newly born deer, she explored her freedom at first cautiously, but as her confidence gave her self-assurance, she began to feel at ease to wander.

This I grasped only from the conscientious insights she allowed me to reflect upon. I learned, also, that she has an elder sister. Controversially, perhaps, she does not want to marry in line with recommendations, but out of love. After school, she wants to go to university and pursue a hectic career in journalism.

Before me, she appears as a young woman, although her emotions have matured beyond her years. At first, when unacquainted, people may have been discouraged by her hijab, as the modern connotations that have developed seem to lead to the cry 'terrorist'. Her hijab, however, modestly hides her beauty and strength, which prevails despite the recurring abuse. Its current absence suggests to me that perhaps England today is not accepting of change.

I ask her again about her past, between her early years in England and the present. The Najwa that I know, or think I know, now seems an incomplete portrait. Smiling in her entrancing way, she turned to me. The serene glimmer in her eye told me that the mystery would remain, at least for now.

Sheridan McWilliam

The Language Assistant's Tale

Every year, around thirty young people come to live in Lincolnshire to work as foreign language assistants in our secondary schools whilst languages students at British universities go out to other countries to help their schools teach English. Most of those coming to Lincolnshire are from France, Germany, Spain and other Spanish speaking countries, though we also get a small number from China and Russia. How they get on during their year here is determined largely by the quality of the welcome they receive. This piece is based on an interview with a French languages assistant.

Imagine leaving your country. Without your family, away from your friends – all alone, knowing nobody. How would you feel? Dominique Pestourie not only had to leave her loved ones, but also her way of life and adjust to an entirely new culture: en Angleterre. At the tender age of 22, Dominique set off on a journey that would change her view of life forever. The ferry's passengers disembarked after the journey from Calais to Dover, across what she calls "La Manche" and we call the "English Channel." Dominique is, as you may have gathered, French. 'J'ai été charmée' was her comment to us; a faraway look clouding her vision and a broad smile illuminating her features.

First impressions of Dominique would probably not have drawn us to her; her style does not immediately reflect her dynamic personality and she comes across as a shy and quiet individual. Dressed in monochrome black, hair pulled back and carrying a bag with the motto "Le Chat Noir," her dark eyes expressed all that we felt inside: anxiety and apprehension. We were definitely worried about the task ahead. Curious as we were about her story, it is never easy to ask personal questions of a near stranger, as we have discovered. Her responses to the first few questions were initially hesitant, short and vague but soon enough both her shyness and our trepidation evaporated.

Conversation had to be roughly translated into the other's native language for easier understanding, but it truly is amazing how much one can discover about a person over a short space of time despite language boundaries. As we spoke to her we could read her body language, and she ours, so if there was a lull in conversation due to a lack of understanding we could soon pick up with some dramatic actions. We were both glad she had taken an English degree - we would have had much more difficulty with a lesser linguist.

Many things, naturally, are different in our country. We asked her about the first things that came across to her as different and she paused, thinking how to phrase her answer, before listing three points: our culinary habits, our popular customs and the school system. A general answer, perhaps; deliberately devoid of opinion so as not to offend, along with many of the things Dominique told us. What she particularly likes about our country is the "openness and tolerance of its people," which we hope we helped convey with our demeanours.

Mme Pestourie, we discovered, found it especially hard to leave her family. With three sisters (she neither oldest nor youngest) she misses them a great deal, but makes sure to contact her siblings and parents as often as possible to make the move easier for all of them. Although only here for a year, it is still hard and neither of us can really comprehend staying away from home for such a sustained period of time - the most either has experienced is ten days away. Dominique obviously feels the strain of the separation, as despite her lack of distinct opinion, she responds to our question 'Considérez-vous vivre en Angleterre?' ('Would you consider living in England?') with a brief, blunt almost, answer of 'No, I wouldn't consider living here.'

The French are not so different from the English. As nations, we have both found the other open to co-operation: on a small scale, with our interview of Dominique and with French exchanges and on a larger scale, with things like the Channel Tunnel and our alliance during the two major wars of the twentieth century, despite hereditary rivalry.

The French, as a people, work the same way as the English and meeting with Dominique has made us realise this. We have found the experience of talking to her enlightening and motivating – we both intend to learn more about the culture, and Dominique is going to help us, through an exchange of letters with a school in France. We are, after all, one species. Why should language separate us?

Rebecca Bates and Mollie Turner

Dear Morteza

Dear Morteza,
How are you doing in England? All is well, here in Iran and
everyone sends their regards. Thank you for replying to my
previous letter about my visit to England. I have spoken to the
rest of the family and they have approved of my visit becoming a
little more permanent. My arrangements are yet to be finalised,
for I wish to ask you first if everything we discussed is in check
with your plans. I look forward to your reply.

With regards
Mojtaba

The year was 1975, and Mojtaba had set foot on English soil for
the first time. All of the planning and waiting and finalising seemed
like a distant memory. The day had finally arrived. Mojtaba had
arrived in England.

Exhausted from the seven-hour journey from Tehran to
Heathrow, Mojtaba was not in the best of moods, but he pushed
aside his tired state of mind and instead anticipated what the next
six months were going to bring.

Collecting his luggage, he then proceeded to make his way
through arrivals. A sea of multi-coloured placards and laminated
pieces of card with relatives' and friends' names plastered on
them instantly hit Mojtaba's eyes. He scanned the crowd, taking
in his surroundings, and eventually found his brother. A feeling
of familiarity overwhelmed him. He was beginning to feel out of
place, but seeing his brother Morteza again, had reassured him he
was doing the right thing.

'…Are you sure?'

'Certain. It's final. We are now the official owners of our new
business, *Mona Lisa!*'

Exhilarated from the good news, Mojtaba thought back to when
he had first arrived in England and how far he had come since

then. Finishing his course at university had finally given him the incentive he had needed to look for something new. The fact that he and two of his close friends were business partners was something of a reassurance. Finally, things were starting to fall into place.

All that education gone to waste… what am I going to do?

Mona Lisa had been successfully running for four years now, but the exhilaration Mojtaba had once felt had left him, and instead a hollow feeling of emptiness occupied him. Things had been looking up. Business was thriving and customer numbers were swiftly growing. Although the business was successful, Mojtaba could not ignore the gnawing feeling of doubt any longer. All of those years spent studying and working hard to achieve good grades seemed like they had all gone to waste now. What was he using them for? Three years after opening the pizza shop, Mojtaba had bought his friend's shares in the business to become the sole owner and manager of *Mona Lisa*. From the exterior things couldn't have looked better but Mojtaba felt that he needed to follow his gut instinct and put his education to use. After all, the reason why Mojtaba had moved to England was to further his education. He had left behind a loving family to come and stay with his brother, Morteza.

Things had gone so well that his visit lasted a lot longer than six months, becoming, in fact, six years.

Teaching was something Mojtaba never thought he would end up choosing as a career. It had never crossed his mind, for he was the type of person who enjoyed learning rather than teaching. Nevertheless, teaching others to learn was one of the most rewarding things he had done. His time as a maths and electronics engineering lecturer was something Mojtaba enjoyed a lot.

Even through all of the uncertainty and doubt, it had never crossed his mind to give up and go back to Iran. Opportunities lay in England, and Mojtaba was determined to become a successful and fulfilled person. Moving to England at the young age of 18 was a life-changing decision. Today he still lives in the town of Grantham with his wife, 15-year-old daughter and 13-year-old son. *Mona Lisa* has been open for 18 successful years now, and is still running, and hopefully will do so for many years to come.

By Shahrzod Hashemi-Parast

Regina

Starting a new school is never easy, but can you imagine beginning a new school in a totally different country, culture and language? Well this is what Regina had to do when her parents split up and her mother and three siblings were forced to migrate to England while her brother and father stayed in Latvia. Ten people from my year group had the opportunity to go to St. Mark's School, Lincoln, to interview foreign kids our age, and the girl I met was 17 years old and moved here just three months ago.

We all stepped out of the minibus, suddenly sticking together like glue because we had just arrived in this strange and unfamiliar environment. Intimidated by the students, we made our way down countless corridors to the room where we were to meet the foreigners. When we entered the room, all of us gathered in the seats to the left-hand side of the classroom; the St. Mark's students on the right-hand side. The teachers stood in the middle ready to pair us up.

Regina. That was her name, but I thought it was Gina for a while. She peered over at my piece of paper and saw that I'd written her name down incorrectly and so she repeated her name. People say things come in threes, so after asking her a third time to repeat it, I wrote down what I heard and hoped I'd spelt it right, and I had. I felt slightly uncomfortable when I first sat down next to Regina, because in my school, only a very small percentage of the pupils are from another country, so mixing with different cultures is very alien to me, which I am ashamed to admit. After a few minutes, though, we were more at ease with each other and we were able to maintain a conversation.

Latvia. That is the country she comes from. Yes, I'd heard of it, but to be honest I didn't know much about it, so had to ask many simple questions about the weather – which she told me was humid and warm in the summer, and freezing in the winter – and population – which is about 2,250,000. After researching when I went home, I discovered that Latvia has the highest abortion rate in the world. In these circumstances you might think that no one would have a large family, but Regina's mother has given birth to five children. Now her mother is working eight-hour days at a factory to provide for her family. Regina comes from a place called Riga in Latvia, and she told me she lived near a big sea, which she misses. But apart from that, she appears to prefer living in England. Apparently the people at school in Latvia weren't very pleasant, but here she was welcomed and everyone was kind to her, especially the teachers.

Seventeen. She and I are a similar age, growing and experiencing teenage life, but it appeared that our lives are quite different. My parents split up when I was eight years old, and however hard that was, it's fine now as I visit Dad at least once a week. He lives only ten minutes away; her dad lives on the other side of the world. All my friends are English and we all speak the same language, but in Regina's group of friends, there are some Russian and Polish girls, as well as people from Afghanistan, and England. At St. Mark's School there is a large variety of cultures and races, and Regina definitely isn't the only pupil who has moved here recently from a totally different country. Racism appears to be a huge issue in this day and age according to the newspapers and television, but Regina settled in splendidly in her new school and home, and people treated her pleasantly. She spoke very highly of this country and frequently praised the manners and friendliness of the people she has met in England. She also talked about how beautiful Lincoln is, and she told me she often loves to simply walk around the city and admire the views and breathe in the fresh aromas, as Latvia is highly polluted. I felt a pang of guilt because I have so many luxuries which I take for granted like a lovely house, and a great education, and I've grown up in a wonderful country.

At school, Regina studies maths, Russian, ICT, tourism and English. When she's older she would like to use travel and tourism in a career. I think this is ironic, because she's experienced life in a different country and has discovered England is better, so I'd assumed that she'd want to stay in England when she's older. The hardest thing for Regina about being in this school is the fact that she's not only learning the subjects, like most of the other pupils, but she's learning a different language too, so it's doubly difficult. It's like my maths teacher teaching me a lesson in German, and me having to understand what she's telling me as well as doing the maths. That thought scares me enough to understand how hard it must be for Regina, and how it's a constant battle to achieve. Sometimes Regina really wants to say something, but her English lets her down, and she isn't able to communicate what she means, which makes me feel sad because I speak fluent English and I can always say whatever I want without having to even think about it, and it'd be horrible to know what you want to say but be unable to find the right way to say it. Out of school, Regina likes swimming, shopping, dancing and listening to music, like any typical teenager, so she had adapted to life very well by the looks of it.

Meeting Regina made me think a lot about myself and my life, and about the simple things I take for granted that she talked about with wonder and admiration. I thought about how England really is a lovely, welcoming and friendly country. When she talked about all the aspects of living in England, I felt proud, and lucky. It was certainly very interesting and eye-opening to meet this girl from Latvia.

Rachel Ram

The Decision

We always hear about immigrants in countries around the world finding safety and solace in the countries of the west, changing their lives forever, and living happily ever after in their new homes.

This is not one of those stories. Things for Kofryna Adamkutė have not ended happily ever after. The barren wastelands and run-down cities of Lithuania may seem like a world away from England, but by leaving all of the things she loved behind, she changed her own life forever.

When I first met Kofryna we did not connect with each other. She was an 18-year-old Lithuanian girl, speaking in broken English, extremely insecure and fervently resistant to leaving her two Polish friends. I was a 15-year-old English boy, having lived here all my life, outgoing, confident and open about myself. I had always been used to people of all races living together, being friends and accepting each other's differences. I can number amongst my friends a Lithuanian, an Irish boy and a Pakistani, and I am happy about this. But the same cannot be said for Kofryna's school.

From the moment I entered the doors I felt a certain tension. We were standing there in our pristine black blazers, our neat shirts and our tightly fastened top buttons and ties, but we were surrounded by kids dressed in thick jumpers, shirts hanging out, ties knotted halfway down their chests. Whispers broke out all around us, and I noticed an enmity between people that I had never experienced before. Aside from the 'normal' pupils, there were small pockets of people scattered around the corridors, quietly receiving disapproving looks from those around them. The rift was totally alien to me. Anyone who seemed different from the norm of the white, British, football-loving or celebrity-gossiping teenager was automatically shunned. I read nervousness and fear on the faces of these 'outcasts'. Every immigrant, whether Eastern European, Asian or African, anyone who was different, seemed to be extremely wary of their own 'freakishness'.

Kofryna's own face reflected this mindset: that if you aren't British you aren't welcome.

Sticking closely to her best friends, two Polish girls, Alenka and Delfina, she told me of her life, her journeys and her homes, of her life in Lithuania, and her life in England.

Kofryna was born in the bustling town of Kaunas in 1990. Life in the Baltic was hard. The cold summers and colder winters meant life was almost unbearable. When she was born, Soviet rule was still in place. The Cold War was drawing to a close, but the cold fist of Moscow, although waning, still held a firm grip over the Eastern world. The Berlin Wall had come down, and as a new wave of independence spread across the world, all of the Baltic States held their breath, waiting to see what a new day would bring.

Kofryna's mother, Andra Adamkienė, was a shopkeeper in the busy centre of Kaunas, working long hours in a dusty, run-down grocery shop, for hardly any money, and with the only thing to look forward to, being to return every night to a pokey apartment in one of Kaunas's many tower blocks of flats. Her father didn't work.

This life carried on day after day, week after week. As world events occurred around her, Kofryna continued as normal. She didn't care that the USSR had fallen, or that Russia had given independence to thousands of people, from the plains of Latvia and Estonia, to the coasts of the Black Sea, to the steppes of Kazakhstan, to the busy cities of Eastern Germany. She didn't care that Lithuania had freedom at last; she was only concerned with the state of her home. She went to school as she always did. She came home as she always did. She helped her mother in the shop as she always did. No new government could change this. The collapse of communism didn't affect her at all. She was concerned with the more mundane things in life. Learning English in school, thinking about what to have for tea, whether to play with her childhood friends or just to stay at home.

Despite this, Kofryna grew up very quickly. Her worries

turned to the more important things in life, as she, and all of Lithuania's poor, discovered the sad reality of independence. Mass unemployment, recession, poverty. It was almost as bad as when Russia was ruler.

When Kofryna turned 12, she entered secondary school. She began to see a change in the country. Workers were leaving for new countries: America, Germany, France, Spain and, most importantly, England. The parents of her friends were moving from the country abroad, seeking a better life there, no matter what it took.

Thoughts of emigration entered the minds of Kofryna's parents too. It was a few weeks after her twelfth birthday when her parents called her into the living room of their cramped inner-city flat.

'Kofryna,' said her father in Lithuanian, 'sit down. Your mother and I–well–we have something to tell you.'

'We are leaving to work in England,' said her mother in no more than a whisper. Kofryna could just see that her mother's eyes were filling with tears through her golden veil of hair.

Those words. 'We are leaving to work in England.'

England.
Anglija.
Although it was only a few hundred miles away, England seemed worlds away. The green fields of England, from what she had heard, were nothing like Lithuania's cold mountains and plains. The cold Russian winds that carried nothing but fear from Moscow and Kiev to Kaunas, were nothing like the warm, luscious sunshine that graced the British countryside. Britain had everything–jobs, opportunity, freedom; they had stood as a beacon for the freedom of Lithuania, and the Great British hope had always filled the hearts of the Lithuanian people. To go there would be a dream. However, there was one thing about England that made Kofryna think. It wasn't losing her friends. It wasn't moving schools. It wasn't even having to learn a whole new language and culture.

England just wasn't home.

'Well,' said Kofryna quietly, 'will we all have to leave?'

'Papa and I will be leaving in November,' replied her mother, stifling a sob. 'You'll be living with Aunt Rasa and Uncle Mykolas in Panevėžys and when we've found a job, and a home, and a school, you'll come and join us.'

'But what if–but I–well–I–don't want–I don't want to go,' muttered Kofryna in vain.

'No buts, Kofryna,' said her father sternly. 'Mama and I have decided.'

'Don't–you care about what–what I think?' pleaded Kofryna.

'Kofryna, it is decided,' interrupted Papa.

Kofryna looked at her mother in a final plea, but Mama just turned away, unable to meet Kofryna's tear-stained gaze.

About three months later, the small 12-year-old stood on a lonely platform in a station on the edge of Kaunas, waiting for the train to Panevėžys. When she looked down the far-stretching railroad she could just see the train that was at that moment carrying her parents to Kaunas airport to fly them to England. They had left with no more than just a peck on the cheek and a tearful goodbye from her mother.

As the train vanished into the distance, another rumble of the tracks heralded the arrival of another train–her carriage to her new life in Panevėžys. The train screeched to a halt, like a mechanical fanfare for this insignificant suburban girl. Once the door opened she picked up her suitcase and scrambled up the stairway. After struggling to place her case on the luggage rack, she nestled herself in a seat next to the window. There were only a few other people in her car. Opposite sat a man who seemed to be in his late forties. He wore a large fur hat, the type that wouldn't go amiss in the streets of Cold War Moscow. A few rows behind her was a large family made up of a worn-out mother, a frustrated looking father, and a horde of screaming children. As the train rattled further north, the snow began to fall, and with every small frozen flake the five or six children's excitement grew and mounted into a chorus of laughter and screaming, like a multitude of dying cats. An old woman who looked a lot like Kofryna's Baba–grandmother sat by the door, her chin bearing the knot of her headscarf, her handbag perched gracefully on her lap.

The fields and mountains turned whiter. The snowdrifts piled by the side of the tracks looked like towering white cliffs flanking the roads. Three hours passed until the tallest spires of Panevėžys appeared in the far distance, and when the train eventually pulled up by the station, Kofryna took a deep breath and stepped off.

It would be wrong to say that Rasa and Mykolas were unwelcoming to their niece; in fact, on the contrary, she was very welcome. She bunked in with her cousin Jurate, who was a little older than her, around 15, and played for the rest of the holidays with Jecis, another cousin around her own age. But she missed Kaunas, and Mama and Papa, and her school friends. After a month her heart was yearning for her parents, but she had no news until late December.

Christmas was a simple affair. There was just Kofryna, Jurate, Jecis, Rasa, Mykolas and her cousin, Jurgi, Jurate's stepbrother who had just moved to England himself with his family. She received a jumper from her aunt and uncle, and some chocolates from her cousins, but the most welcome gift was a letter from her parents. Her dad had found a job in a small factory in a town in England called Lincoln, and Mother had been house-hunting and had discovered a cheap house around the corner from a school, not too close to the centre of Lincoln, but not too far away. It was also close to a supermarket where Mama was working part-time until things at home had settled down. The letter said she would come to join them in August, a few weeks before her 13th birthday.

The next few weeks and months flew by in no time at all. School went on as normal, but Aunt Rasa had thought it would be a good idea for Kofryna to learn English, so she paid for a private tutor, a Mr Kairys. Although he was nice and knew a few pieces of basic English, Kofryna had an inkling that there was more to the language than he was teaching her (or knew).

When the day came, Kofryna was a cocktail of emotions. The entire family took her to the airport. Jecis and Jurate were upset to see her go, but Kofryna assured them both that she would see them soon. Uncle Mykolas sorted out the tickets and boarding passes, and at the gate Aunt Rasa saw her off with a big kiss.

Once again the little girl was on her own. She passed through immigration and passport control. She passed through security and entered a vast hallway, filled with strangers. Desperately she turned, hoping to catch a sight of her family, but the sea of passport booths, X-ray machines, security guards and metal detectors all blocked the view to the gate and beyond. She took a deep breath and stepped towards the gate. Following the sign for departures, she frantically chased through the mêlée of tourists, commuters and businessmen. They all milled around her, jabbering in every language on earth: Lithuanian, Russian, Polish, English, German, Estonian, Latvian, Czech. The rampant footsteps of children venturing on their great holiday to some tropical island, the sluggish ones of those just returning, the great beehive of the airport was buzzing with chatter and noise, but she eventually reached her waiting area and slumped into the nearest chair.

When her plane was finally called, she scrambled for her bags and rushed to the door to find her seat. Showing her ticket and passport, she hurried along the corridor to the plane; she struggled to place her case on the luggage rack and then she nestled into her seat next to the window.

After the customarily irritating safety talk, a rumble from the engine heralded the departure of Kofryna's carriage to her new life in Lincoln. The plane roared, a deafening whirligig of noise, like a mechanical fanfare for this insignificant immigrant girl. The aeroplane launched into the air as the fields and mountains below melted and merged into one another. The sea soon stretched into a carpet below the wings, while she silently flew over the Baltic. Denmark seemed to be a tiny bump on the minuscule patchwork quilt that was the German coast. Several hours had passed when the pilot announced on the speakers that the cliffs of Dover were just visible in the distance. Kofryna leaned to look out of the window, to see great walls of white that seemed to be no more than snowdrifts piled high on the seashore, when actually they were great barricades obstructing any passage from land or sea. Ominous storm clouds lingered above the plane and reached off into the horizon, framing these natural defences like a sinister spirit. If first impressions were anything to go by, England wouldn't be the welcoming home Kofryna had thought it would be. She was right.

The opening days of life in Britain were fine enough. Seeing Mama and Papa again was the best thing she could ask for, but it was September and she had to begin English school. She felt that there was something wrong with her neat school jumper and tie. Her timid footsteps carried her across the road and through the menacing school gates that morning without a word. Inside the corridors, stares and dirty looks were thrown at her. Struggling to get through the crowded corridors, with people hustling past her and knocking her already shaking hands, she attempted to read the map to reach her form room. Finally she reached the room, entered, and sat near the back, attempting to disregard the stares of disapproval from the natives around her.

Kofryna could not have felt worse about herself that day. Being introduced to the class by an overly patronising woman called Mrs Smallbone meant that she ceased to be 'new girl', and was now 'immigrant girl', a title which came along with fewer smiles than 'new girl'. No one talked to her at all before lunchtime, and even then she found herself sat in a corner of a bustling canteen. Her head buried in an English dictionary and her attention focussed on her lasagne, she hardly noticed when two other girls sat down opposite her. Timidly she looked up to see a pair of smiling blonde heads staring straight at her.

'Hello?' Kofryna said apprehensively; Would these be two more English cows ready to poke fun at her hair, or her shoes, or her accent?

'Hello...... my name...... Delfina...... this...... this is Alenka...... we...... Polski,' said the taller of the two.

Kofryna felt as if a huge weight had been lifted from her shoulders. Poles! Other immigrants, other 'freaks', other outsiders.

'Kofryna, Kofryna Adamkutė. Lithuaniski.' she said at last,

smiling happily.

The three of them had a lengthy conversation, some of it in broken English, with snippets of basic Lithuanian or simple Polish intermingled with expressive hand gestures. They didn't let on, but all three of the girls knew that they had found some lifelong friends, and for the first time in months Kofryna was truly happy.

'Oi, foreigners!!!' came a voice from across the food hall. The three friends' heads turned to see a group of young men, no more than 16, standing a few metres away. 'Shift! You're in our seats!'

'Sorry…,' stammered a taken aback Kofryna, 'We'll… um… move…'

'Don't you dare talk to me, you dirty cow,' snapped the tallest boy. Kofryna slowly walked past him, not meeting his loathing gaze, but as she passed his hand shot out from his pocket, causing her lunch and tray to erupt into the air and clatter onto the floor.

Kofryna's head was spinning, she could see faces laughing, the room around her became streaked as her eyes filled with tears, she was stumbling, her eyes were so filled that she couldn't see a thing, her feet hit the smashed plate on the floor, which slid beneath her… and all she knew was that she was falling. When her back hit the floor she didn't dare to open her eyes. The laughter was still ringing in her ears; she could feel the boys' spit hitting her face like a malicious shower, mixing with her tears to create a cocktail swilling on her cheeks. Her mind was a mixture of feelings: self-pity, anger, hate, all culminating in her new notion about her new life. It was going to be hell.

Kofryna hated her life at that school. No one except for the other foreigners talked to her. No one acknowledged her existence. No one really cared that much. She has grown up a lot since she left Lithuania. She knows now how much better her new life is; after going home to Kaunas once, she realises that Britain is home now. It's not that she doesn't miss Lithuania. She does, but her life in Lincoln is one with an income, and friends in the same town. She couldn't go back now. She did well in her GCSEs, a few As, some Bs and a couple of Cs tided her over into sixth form, and she now wants to go into tourism, like many of her friends. She now stays oblivious to the outside, because in a year's time she will never have to go to that school again - she will be able to live again.

I do not think I will see Kofryna again. When she saw me she didn't connect or smile. She is still cocooned inside her tiny shell, one of defence, and after her life here, I don't think she will ever truly trust the British again. She has faced too much segregation. Too much hatred. Too much hiding from the world. She will go on hiding, and the world will keep on turning around her. But she's happy - happy staying with Alenka and Delfina, happy living the way she always has and always will: a little girl, wandering in a great big world.

Patrick Campbell

Anla

I sat, nervously fiddling with the pen cap, at my kitchen table. Thoughts were racing rapidly within my head, although none of them were quite fitting together. The nerves were getting to me as I started to wonder how she would react to my interrogation. My mind started to wander. A large, powerful woman entered the room alongside my mother. Immediately I felt incredibly small, as though she could flatten me under her short, stubby thumb. I piped up, wanting to end this as soon as possible. I watched her face as I dictated the first of my many questions. My voice grew quieter as I watched a crimson shade spread across her face. She swept a sleeve across her brow.

The trance was soon broken by the sound of my mother's voice and the kitchen door handle creaking slowly downwards. I sat up straight instantly, forcing myself to form a smile, which hopefully would seem warm enough to make someone feel comfortable. My mother gestured her hand towards this woman. She was young and instantly made an impression. I looked at her closely before acknowledging her name. She wore black from head to toe, covering up most of her body. She seemed to have a closed character, reluctant to let others into her life, an elusive young woman. Soft, delicate curls had escaped the scraped-back ponytail, brushing gently against her golden earrings. Anla. I prayed silently, thanking God. She was the total opposite to the woman created in my imagination.

I was reluctant to ask intimate questions, although to my astonishment this woman was able to capture my mind's eye as images formed in front of me from her descriptions.

At only four months Anla had lost her mother, not by chance but by choice; being thrown away by the woman who brought her into this world left Anla to be taken in by charity homes. She was torn away from every home, having to leave behind friends, the only people who understood her, and start all over again. Looking back, it was all just a blur. That a child of such a young age should block out these astonishing memories is hard to believe. Still, she always remembered thinking that the charity homes shouldn't be called 'homes'- in her opinion she defined a home as being a place where you feel you belong, somewhere you feel comforted, safe and surrounded by people who love you and whom you love in return. She travelled across the country over numerous years, until she found her future parents. She finally had people to love, and to love her back. She could depend on them, and forget the memories of being rejected by her own flesh and blood. Her foster parents had taken her in. They had no other children, so loved and cared for her the only way they could, as if she were their own.

Anla was 16. In 1990, when the Russians had invaded her home land of Lithuania, Vilnius was smothered with violence and terrified screams. Tanks freely roamed the city streets, gunshots being fired aimlessly. Life had changed dramatically; even occasions that were thought to be full of laughter, smiles and joy were stripped of their happiness. Anla explained the times when she was happiest: 'Happy New Year!' she said with a smile. Gifts exchanged hands alongside smiles of gratitude; music filled the room, while the tipsy elders encouraged reluctant relatives to dance; a silence spread across the crowd while fireworks filled the sky with colourful lights. She described enthusiastically the celebration that occurred without fail every year, until the Russians had turned their beloved country into a land full of terror. Anla could not play along the streets for the dread of being terrorised. She was living in fear.

In the light of everything she had experienced, Anla had to move. After settling in for ten years with her foster parents, they had pressed it onto her to emigrate, to find a job. She knew she had to go so she could find herself a better home, in a country free of violence and the terror she experienced daily: she could then restart her life. Perhaps she could forget the memories that might scar her for life. The experience should have shaken her, leaving the only country she had ever known to find a new, alien home. Anla found strength in seeing the positive: it was her first time flying and she loved it.

Stories of other people's lives may interest you, although some may bore you. However, whichever it may be, some people's lives can capture your heart and make you sit still for hours on end, yearning to hear more of their incredible journey through life. Rarely do you have this opportunity to absorb the tales of wonderful characters.

I watched Anla traipse slowly away from here, down the drive. So many people would notice her, but none would wonder who she was. She peered left, then right and then stepped off the path and began to cross, but the onlookers wouldn't realise the hardships she had endured. She walked around the corner and out of sight. No one would remember the day they caught a glance of Anla.

Amelia Dray

The Tale of the Lithuanian Girl

The room went silent as she spoke. An eerie atmosphere lingered after she had finished. She told her father of the conversation she and her mother had had on the phone earlier that day. Her father began to turn a shade of white, standing out against the vibrant curtains behind him. His eyes widened and his face held a blank expression, but yet it spoke a thousand words. A small, delicate tear slid down his cheek. It was there for only a moment before he brushed it away in anger, as if he was hoping he could do the same with the daughter who was about to leave him forever.

'I'm so sorry Dad,' she whispered silently to him with as much sincerity as she could muster.

'But why Elena? You are the only thing I have. I have fought to keep you safe, keep a roof over your head - and this is how you repay me?' he shouted out at her, flinging the little table her mother had sent them from England across the room as if it was weightless. He jumped up from his seat and dashed over to her. His eyes looked as if they were emitting the fires of hell. He stopped in front of her face and gazed into her innocent young eyes.

'Just go, Elena. I don't want to see your face. I will ring your mother to arrange your journey to England, and after that I never want to see either of you again.' He looked away from her as he said this, as if he couldn't stand the sight of her.

'But, Father, I didn't want it to be like this. I only want a better life...' said Elena, her eyes full of tears that she tried to hold back.

'No, just stop Elena,' he interrupted, 'as far as I am concerned you are no daughter of mine!' And with this final sentence, he rushed from the room. All Elena heard after that was the slam of the door.

She waited all night for her father to come back to her. She felt scared and unwanted. She knew that she had betrayed him, but she thought that it was for the best. After all, who in this small village in Lithuania doesn't want a better life? Elena knew that she could be living in worse conditions than she was now, but apart from her father there was nothing to keep her here. The town consisted of three supermarkets and one small clothes shop full of old, pre-owned clothes that smelt like the flat of the old lady next door. The buildings were antique-looking, the rusty, grey paint peeling off more and more everyday. The windows were dirty and looked out on the tedious landscape that consisted of lifeless trees and plants. Her father worked in one of these buildings for a company that packaged goods that were exported to other countries in large, robust ships down at a nearby port.

School was hard for Elena as she didn't have many friends. It's not that Elena didn't want to make friends, it was just that the people at her school were so different from her that she didn't want to have to change her personality to fit in. There seemed to be a stereotype that if you weren't into make-up and boys then you weren't like them, but if you relished reading a book or visiting museums, then you were a geek, a nerd that people couldn't be seen talking to. You were a nobody, invisible and transparent to the people around, with the only exception being when they wanted to make fun of the way you dressed or mock you if you answered questions in class. In Elena's mind *they* were the nobodies; the people who on their outer shell portrayed a feeling of power and presence but on the inside were frightened and scared of the truth – that they and people like Elena were more alike than they thought.

So, overall, life in Lithuania was hard, and she decided it had to change. That's when Elena's mother had phoned, begging her to come and live with her and her boyfriend where she currently lived in England, in a place called Lincoln. She made it sound like some sort of magical land compared to the bland and tedious village in Lithuania. She described its bustling city centre, full to the brim with clothes shops that weren't replete with pre-owned clothes. The small cafés and restaurants, full of people, who warmly welcomed her to the city. Her mother made this place sound perfect, like a home.

That's when Elena realised she had to go there. But that meant she had to leave her father. She felt bad for leaving him but she couldn't blame herself any longer for her parents' separation. She knew it was his fault. Elena remembered when it all started six years ago. She had awoken suddenly to her father's angry voice, so loud that it vibrated the paper-thin walls around her. A crashing sound could be heard and then there was silence. A cold and frightening feeling had taken over her body, sending shivers, it seemed, to her very soul.

The next day her mother walked into her bedroom to wake her. Elena looked at her face and gasped at the ghastly purple bruise that sat on her once red, rosy cheek. She gazed in horror at the sight of this dominant feature that stuck out on her mother's delicate face, overpowering the beautiful features that she had once possessed.

'Mother, what happened?' quizzed Elena.

'It does not matter – it was nothing, I… I slipped on the floor yesterday and bashed my head. Now go on, get ready for school, you will be late.' She smiled at her daughter, which immediately diverted Elena's gaze from the nasty bruise. She could gaze at that smile all day; it made her feel happy and loved.

'Do I have to go to school today?' quizzed Elena, gazing at her mother with her puppy-dog eyes.

'Yes, of course,' replied her mum, laughing as she spoke.

'OK' said Elena, and she shuffled over to the wardrobe to get changed.

'Elena, you do know that I love you, don't you?' asked her mum.

'Yes, of course Mum. Why?' she asked, feeling a little confused.

'I just thought I'd check,' she replied. She walked over to Elena and kissed her on her forehead. She held her close to her chest and Elena smiled. She hugged back, gripping tight like she never wanted to let go. Her mother pulled away and walked towards the door, only turning back to say 'I love you' one last time and look deep into her daughter's eyes once more. Elena noticed a small, almost invisible tear slide elegantly down her cheek, but then her mother had turned away and left. That was weird, thought Elena, it was almost as if she was saying goodbye, but then she remembered she had school and began pulling on her scratchy school uniform.

Later that day, Elena opened her front door with a sigh, kicked off her shoes, dumped her bag on their kitchen table and sat grumpily on one of the old, creaky chairs. School had been tedious, as usual. She had walked through the school gates to see other children her age running up to their friends, exchanging stories of what had happened to them during the weekend. But Elena had no one to run to, no one to tell stories to or gossip with. Instead she crept up to the big, oak doors trying to be invisible to the glaring eyes, the echoing laughs. She eventually reached the safety of the school and hid in the cloakroom till the bell went. Each lesson she walked in to the room and tried to find a table close to the back with no one sat at it. She would look enviously at the other children who were laughing and joking with friends, at the boys and girls who glanced at each other across the room, sending notes with big love hearts, their initials inside. She wondered to herself when she would get friends or even a boyfriend? Maybe when she moved up to the bigger school she could make new friends and find a boy? She smiled to herself as she faded away into a daydream. Here she was the popular one, the one that people envied, the one that the boys fancied, the one who got to pick on people like the real her. Oh what she would give to be that girl! Each lesson she dreamed of being that girl in that world, but in the real world she was oblivious to the books being opened, the writing on the board, the questions being asked. Then the bell went and her world evaporated, dissolving into the back of her mind. She ran across the playground to shouts of 'Geek' and 'Nerd' but she didn't care. She just wanted to get home.

She came back from her reflection on that day's events and jumped up from the chair. She ran off to her mum's bedroom, but her mother wasn't there. She tried the sitting room, but she wasn't there. With a last, desperate hope she checked her own bedroom, but again, she wasn't there. This was strange to Elena; her mother was always there when she came home from school, as her mother didn't have a job. She pondered the possibility that her mother had gone to the shops and concluded that this must be the reason for her absence. So she lay down on her squeaky bed and began to read her favourite book, *Alice in Wonderland*. She had just got to her favourite part when the front door slammed, sending particles of dust drifting from the old cabinet in the corner. She placed her book back on the floor and waited for her mother to come to her room, ready to explain why she had not been there when Elena had come home. But she was shocked to find that her father was standing in her doorway, tears flooding down his face.

'Father, what's wrong?'

'It's your mother,' he sobbed. 'She's left us!'

'Why?' gasped Elena, trying to take in what her father had just told her.

'I don't know, Elena,' he shouted, 'maybe it was because of you.'

'Why, what have I done?' spluttered Elena, still reeling from the news.

'Maybe you were a disappointment to her, maybe you weren't good enough,' he bellowed, spit spraying from his mouth. He gripped the doorframe as he spoke, like he was trying to hold back his pain.

'I don't understand, Father, I thought she loved us,' Elena sobbed, tears streaming down her face.

'Well she obviously didn't love us enough, she's taken all her clothes and gone forever. All she left was this note.' He wiped away his tears and as he spoke, flung the note towards her and left the room. Elena pounced on the note, scraping her knee as she did so, but she didn't care. The note read…

My Dearest Elena and Gustaf

I am so sorry to be doing this to you, but I can't live this life any longer. Each day I wake next to a husband who I'm afraid will hurt me if I do something wrong. I can't live with this fear any more, it's engulfing me and taking over my life. The only thing keeping me here is my beloved daughter, Elena. It pains me so much to do this to you, it's breaking my heart, but I have to. When you are older, Elena, you will understand, and maybe one day I can see you again. I know you will be angry with me for not taking you too, but this is too dangerous for you and I will not risk it. I'm going to live with a friend in England. I've left you both half of my savings; it's not much, but it's all I can afford to give.

Elena, I hope you know I love you dearly, and each and every day I will miss you so much I'm afraid it will be the death of me. I have left you something under your bed that I hope you will keep. I love you so much, darling.
Love Margreet

Elena looked at the paper, stained with her mother's tears, and she sobbed. She felt as if her heart had been ripped out and thrown away. The pain consumed her body and engulfed her soul. Her tears were cold and endless, the very thought that there was no one here to wipe them away made her cry even more. Then she remembered about the present under her bed. She scrambled over, wiping away her tears as she went and reached under the bed. She felt something soft and pulled it out. A note lay on top, which read:

My dearest daughter Elena
  Love you forever, sweetheart
Mum x

She gazed at the present for a while and stroked the paper. Then she finally slowly unwrapped the paper. Inside lay her mother's wedding dress. Elena used to sneak in to her parents' bedroom and look wondrously at it. It was the most beautiful dress she had ever seen. It was the colour of luxurious white clouds, as if the material had been shaped from them. The beads were made of pearls and hung delicately from the fabric, the veil draped elegantly over the back. Tears came flooding back to her and she clung on to the dress, pressing her nose to the creased fabric and inhaling that sweet smell, her mother's scent. She sobbed into the dress for hours, only stopping occasionally to try and wipe away the stream of tears that flooded her face. It hurt so much to cry, but she could not help it. This was it, her mother had left her, and she wasn't coming back.

Elena returned to the room after reliving her memories. All these thoughts had made her decide. She had to leave her father and Lithuania. She didn't belong here, and the people around her knew it. She could no longer live with a man who had pushed away the people who were most important to him. She rushed off to her room, stamping on the stairs as she did so, causing the little old lady next door to scream out about the noise, but Elena did not care. When she reached her room she paced over to the old wardrobe that took up most of one wall, wrenched open the doors and began to gather up the clutter inside into an old suitcase. After 30 minutes she was packed and ready to leave. Just as she was about to reach for the handle of the front door, another hand beat her to it from the other side and pushed it open. Her father stepped inside and closed it behind him. He turned to face her; his eyes looked dry and empty as if they'd been crying all night. His face was pale and his skin clung to the jutting bones, making him look old and lifeless.

'Father, I was just about to leave,' Elena muttered, not daring to make eye contact.

'I can see that,' he replied. His breath stank of alcohol. 'Here's some money for the flight. I managed to get you one for today: your mother will meet you in England.'

He passed her a crinkled envelope that contained her money.

'I guess this is it, then,' she said, and reached for the door handle.

'Goodbye, Father.'

She walked away from him, from the house that she had grown up in, the house that held so many precious memories and so many horrific ones. The suitcase dragged behind her like a huge weight holding her back. Her knees felt weak and her heart was pumping so hard she was afraid it might burst. She had this horrible feeling, as though she wanted to cry, that felt as if it was burning a hole in her chest. But she persisted and reached the taxi that she assumed her father had phoned to fetch her. A fat bald man stepped out of the taxi. He had a cigarette protruding from his mouth and wore a tight pair of black trousers and a shirt that looked a few sizes too small. His moustache trickled over his top lip and daintily brushed his bottom one as he spoke.

'You can put your bags in the boot,' he grunted. And with that he heaved himself back in the front, causing the car to lean slightly to the left. She had a struggle to lift the suitcase into the boot, but she managed. She took one last look at the house and stepped into the car. It pulled away and she left her street, her town… and arrived at a very old-looking airport that smelt peculiar. She paid the driver and wheeled her suitcase into the waiting area.

'Flight 107 to Heathrow now boarding,' announced a middle-aged woman with a gravely voice. This was it, the start of her new life. She made her way to the gate and took one last look out of the window. This was not where she belonged, she said to herself. She smiled and thought of the life she was going to have with her mother in Lincoln. Her heart jerked as she thought of her poor father all alone, but she had to get away and live her life. She decided she would phone him when she reached Lincoln. And with that she set off down towards the plane, a grin on her face, ready for the journey ahead, ready to become an immigrant.

Bethany Rendall

Who Is She?

We walked hesitantly into the interview room. A small girl sat at the end of the table, head bowed, as if awaiting harsh punishment. I sat down, trying my best to ease the tension. The atmosphere was edgy. Attempting to break the silence, I summoned up the courage to ask the first question. 'So Jadvyga, where did you come from, where were you born?' A look of confusion swept across the girl's face. An interpreter whispered in Jadvyga's ear. She had turned to me, and muttered, as if unwilling to share her story. 'Lithuania. A year, my mother, she...' Even though what she had said came in pidgin English, it was clear from her expression that she was uneasy about retelling the events. I was unsure as to whether her problem was the difference of languages, or that she was simply hesitant about answering my question.

Throughout the interview I struggled to understand what Jadvyga was trying to tell me. As she was apprehensive, the dates, tenses and order of events she described were jumbled, and the interview was like building up a jigsaw; and like many jigsaws, there were vital pieces missing. 'Lithuania. A year, my mother, she wants better life for me and her. My father, he did not. He says stay in Lithuania, don't we dare go.' I realised that I was going to have to tread carefully through the interview, and word my questions well. Jadvyga continued to tell me what happened to her from her interesting, distressing point of view, full of hope, poverty, and turbulent times. 'We had happy life. Me and my mother. Him. He changed it all. He beat.' Holding back my emotions, I tried to stay detached from her story. Some things she described to me would not make sense on paper. I need to describe what happened to Jadvyga as it occurred. The following might sound like something you'd watch on a modern soap opera, but from Jadvyga's experience, it is far from it. As the interview went on, I realised that Jadvyga's life in Lithuania was a complex struggle. 'He would come home, drank too much. We ran away, all we could do.' After listening for a while, it became clear to me the real order of the events. The real events behind Jadvyga's story of her past in Lithuania.

Jadvyga grew up living with her mother. Jadvyga was young, and did not understand her mother's job. Now, aged 15, Jadvyga is glad that she didn't understand. Her mother would go out at night, arriving back at home early in the morning, leaving Jadvyga, a small child, on her own. Her mother didn't do this through choice, clearly, but it was simply the only way she could scrape a living together. From Jadvyga's point of view, she had a happy childhood. She blocked out the bad parts. She remembers the times she and her mother would go to the park for hours, get the bus into their local town, and window shop, imagining what they'd buy if they were 'rich ladies' like the ones they'd seen in the magazines sold outside their small apartment. Clearly she loves her mother with all her heart, and looks up to her, despite now knowing the answers to the many questions she'd ask her mother when she arrived home in the early mornings of the bitter, cold winter.

As Jadvyga grew older, her mother began leaving her on her own for longer periods of time. Sometimes, she would bring home male friends, who needed a place to stay for the night. Jadvyga didn't like it. When Jadvyga felt like she needed some space, she'd go back to the park where she and her mother used to sit for hours on end. She wished it would go back to how it used to be.

She remembered one night, in particular. Jadvyga was sitting watching the small television in her room, which her mother had bought for her eleventh birthday. Her mother had been out a lot in the summer months before she turned 11. She could hear whispers outside her bedroom window. Her mother's voice, along with another, unfamiliar voice. Unusually, her mother popped her head round the door, telling her to come into the living room – there was someone she wanted Jadvyga to meet. Jadvyga tells me that there was a man sitting on the sofa, flicking through a magazine that Jadvyga had bought while her mother was out. At once he looked up as she entered the room. Jadvyga told me that he seemed an ordinary man – short hair, upright posture. He stood up and greeted her. The unfamiliar man had a look of uncertainty in his eyes. Her mother told Jadvyga to sit down. He introduced himself. Jadvyga was still wondering why, of all the men her mother knew, she had decided to introduce this man in particular to her. He looked across to her mother. They smiled. Her mother sat down. What her mother said next, she tells me, had a sort of butterfly effect. A set of dominoes being knocked down one by one. This man, who seemed friendly enough, was Jadvyga's father.

At first, Jadvyga was in a state of shock. She'd been told, from a young age, that she had no father. Whenever she asked about it, she was told she had her mother. That's all that mattered. By now, she'd stopped bothering to ask. There was no point – she never got a straight answer. But there he was, sat on the sofa, your average man – somebody you'd pass on the street without a second glance. She didn't get much of a chance to ask questions, to ask why he hadn't been there all her life. Instead, she just, as normal, soaked in what she'd been told, and accepted it. The man, who she was now told to call 'Dad', moved in. He seemed pleasant. All that mattered to Jadvyga was that he made her mother happy. So she joined in with her mother, opening up to the man, her father. It seemed like this was going to be easy, like the end of a story in the books her mother read her as a child. But it wasn't. Far from it.

As soon as he moved in, her mother didn't leave the house at night. They had nicer clothes. Jadvyga was bought books, a nicer television for her bedroom. Her father had a good job, and they moved out of their small apartment, into a house. All seemed to be going well, until, just like her mother did, he began leaving the house at night time, returning early in the morning. But he was different. You could smell alcohol on his breath, and he was violent. Not too much at first. He threw books, and shouted profanities at her mother when she begged him to stop drinking. But gradually, as the months wore on, it got worse. Her mother started wearing long-sleeved shirts, heavy denim jeans. It wasn't clear at the time – Jadvyga was still only 13. But now looking back, she tells me, this style change wasn't trying out a new look

– it was covering up the beatings her mother received from her now abusive father.

One night, while Jadvyga's father was out, she tells me, her mother poked her head round her door, just like she did that summer night two years before. She was whispering. Jadvyga didn't understand why – nobody lived above, below, or next door any more. Her mother had two duffel bags in her bruised hands: one for Jadvyga, one for her. Jadvyga tells me that at the time, it felt exciting, running away. She felt like she was the actress in her favourite spy film, escaping from the clutches of the enemies that threatened her. She knows now that it must have been incredibly dangerous to run away like that, with her mother. She tells me that it was dark outside as they jumped on the back of a vehicle. This part of her memory was fuzzy. Like I said earlier, she still finds it hard to open up what she had been blocking out of her memory for years. She can remember waking up, and seeing light seeping through the walls of the vehicle they were riding in. She could hear other cars outside, on the road. She woke to the sound of her mother's voice, whispering something that sounded foreign.

The vehicle came to a sudden stop, she told me. A bright light shone on her and her mother – she jokes to me, that she thought something had happened while she and her mother were on the back of the vehicle, and that they were now both in heaven. Far from it actually – they were in Belgium, in the middle of a desolate, freezing-cold car park. It was daytime. She could see, far off, the outline of the sea. Jadvyga tells me she can't remember what happened next; all she knows is what she's been told by her mother: that they walked, until it was dark. They then managed to get on a boat, of some sort, and travel to England.

When they reached England, they went to live in a small apartment, not unlike the apartment they had lived in in Lithuania. It is clear that now, Jadvyga and her mother feel safe. They managed to escape her abusive father. Jadvyga didn't tell me if she'd heard from her father since, but it was clear that she was happy now. She felt safe, and the jigsaw that at first seemed like it had missing pieces was together again. Throughout the interview, it became clear that this amazing story had been locked up inside Jadvyga for years on end, desperate to come out. Now, Jadvyga, a healthy 15-year-old girl living a happy life in England, as close to normal as a person who'd lived a life as hard as hers could be, was free from the past. This, in the end, has made her a stronger person today.

Emily Jenkinson

'We've Decided To Go To England'

Lithuania. Not a lot of people know about it here. In fact not a lot of people are aware that there are a lot of people around who consider it a homeland. 'Eastern European immigrants, ain't they? Stealin' all our jobs!' That's it. Lithuania to a Brit. There's not a lot of empathy is there?

'We've decided to go to England.' There was utter silence around the family gathering. It had been coming, thought Marius, but it was still a shock. You only had to look at his sister's face. No one knew whether to celebrate or cry. It was quite awkward. 'We think that it would be better for all of us,' continued his father. 'In England we can get better opportunities, and better living. It would be good for Marius's and Giedre's education and future. We think that we could be better off there.' Marius went through his father's words in his head. It was great, in theory. In theory. Things are never as simple as that. Marius hardly knew anything about Britain. You wouldn't think it was that different, but it's a whole new culture. A whole new world. Marius sat there, without a clue about what lay ahead.

Driving through the streets of Lazdijai, home, Marius took time to think about his near and distant future. He'd have to get rid of this car first, that was for certain. Old wreck. The grey oppressing tower blocks loomed over the small car like crumbled statues of a broken past. The streets were littered with rubbish and leaves, waiting for the inevitable, smothering snow of the Lithuanian winter. Marius wasn't sad about leaving these things behind. This place was terrible. It was not somewhere Marius would live out of choice. Despite this though, it was not a place Marius would be overjoyed about leaving either. Maybe it was because Lazdijai was part of him. Maybe it was the ominous thought of England, which he knew so little about. Emigrating didn't seem so great now. After living here for 17 years, it was like putting a penguin into the rainforest. His friends had congratulated him, patted him on the back and started joking about the whole thing. Marius had only laughed half-heartedly. It was no joke. Marius had been taking lessons, but he still knew hardly any English – and without English, how would he make friends? How could he fit in? Would he ever? So many questions that seemed to have been neglected by his parents. All had to be faced. Parking the car, he saw all his problems towering higher above him than the blocks of Soviet architecture that surrounded him… 400,000 people emigrate to Britain each year. That's 400,000 people going through almost exactly the same emotions and dilemmas that have dropped, out of nowhere, into Marius's mind. For some the story is worse, a large ball of legal string with a poisoned end. But for all it is a change to the uncertain, and there is nothing more worrying than the thought of uncertain change.

There is something about an airport that really sends negative vibes out to a human being. Firstly, it, like many 'friendly' public places, looks like a hospital, but with more shops. Actually, Vilnius airport looks nothing like a hospital. I looked on the internet. It was very disappointing. For me. However, I'm sure that Marius wasn't really that enthralled by the interior design of the departure lounge. Secondly, there is all the anguish that is sent pulsing around one's mind as if the emotion were some kind of hyperactive headache. However, the dull white walls and the potential thoughts of 'Please don't say that British Airways has messed it all up again!' and 'I hope I don't have to sit next to him for three hours' were far from what Marius was thinking. They say moving house is supposed to be stressful. It's not. Not compared to moving house and country. Marius was wondering deeply whether the decision made by his father was really right. Well, it wasn't that it was the wrong thing to do. England had better housing, better education, better job opportunities with better pay. All that was missing was the giant rainbow and choirs of singing angels. He understood completely why this move was necessary. It was just that he didn't have the will to go. Lithuania had been his life up to now. All his rites of passage had happened there. This is where he had friends, had gone to school, had learned to drive, had grown up. You can't take that to a foreign country, where everything is different and people expect you to do things their way, by the rules of their lifestyle. You can't even bring the furniture.

'It's time we got going,' said his father, some time later. 'Have you got all your papers?' Marius mumbled in agreement, causing his father to reassure him in a method that only parents can do. 'Look it's all fine. Once you're there you will forget all your doubt, and things will be normal once more. Just try to cheer up a bit. It's not as if you're on your own.'

'I know,' replied Marius, rather too quickly and standing up rather too deliberately. And now to the fourth terrible thing about airports: Customs and Immigration. Marius placed his various papers heavily on the desk as his father had done minutes before. Blue visas, green visas, permit papers, family visas; goodness knows what papers all crashed onto the Customs and Immigration desk in a sort of orderly chaos. When Lithuania joined the EU, Marius thought, as the woman behind said desk drearily sorted through the wasted rainforest of forms, that gave Lithuanians a right to freely roam anywhere within the Union's borders. Pah! As long as you had a mountain of official documents proving everything even if it didn't need to be proved or had been proved five times already. Maybe it was because there was a Third World country somewhere whose entire economy was fuelled by producing endless reams of paper. The woman behind the desk handed back these papers along with his passport. She looked like the type of person who hoped a terrorist would come along, just so that she had something interesting to do. After more tedious periods of waiting, the family finally boarded the plane. Marius knew this wouldn't be the last time he would see Lithuania, but he felt like it was.

Marius's first taste of Britain was in short, uninspiring, mostly because of all the reasons concerning airports stated in the last paragraph, and also because the outskirts of London are never exactly picturesque. But this was different. It was like stepping into a new house. Marius felt like such an outsider. Everybody was getting off the plane completely normally. Besides, nothing special had really happened to them. Marius just stood there. He could see mapped out on his sister's face the same look that he felt. This is home.

Well actually, it wasn't. That was in some place far north from here and two train journeys away. Lincoln. A lot of his relatives had moved there a couple of years ago, although, like his recognition of those relatives, his knowledge about the place was quite hazy.

But London was what had to be dealt with at the moment. The first difference Marius noticed between this new foreign world and the Lithuanian one, thousands of miles away, was that here it was raining. He also noticed that, although there were still some, London had a lot fewer flats than Vilnius. The streets were lined instead with semi-detached houses as opposed to the Eastern bloc block housing, where the colour range only extended to a lighter shade of grey. London seemed to be a jumble of houses of every sort organised into rows in a rather messy fashion. However, this change of scenery would simply be forgotten about as the family embarked on the next terrible leg of the journey. It is, to be honest, something to avoid religiously upon arriving in a foreign country and is regarded so badly that it has become a symbol of British pride. I am of course referring to Public Transport.

There are no trains straight to Lincoln. This caused some doubt for Marius because surely Lincoln was supposed to be a city? He looked at all sorts of destinations, listed on endless catalogues, shown on dull television screens. None of them were Lincoln. Surely, thought Marius, a city would be somewhere to go to, not somewhere to stop off on the way to, for example, Leeds – and even then having to change trains, for the purposes of argument, at Newark. In Lithuania a place of that description would, by British standards, be a medium-sized village. That is if they had even connected it in the first place. What was this place supposed to be? In fact Lithuania only has about ten lines, making rail travel a rarely done thing. This, as you can probably see, presents an obvious problem. However, rather boringly, but no less fortunately, the whole expedition took place almost without a glitch. However, that doesn't mean that everything went smoothly. How could it? Getting on the train, the family were inevitably separated. Marius's sister and mother on one side of the aisle and Marius and his father on the other, sitting opposite each other and next to strangers who Marius hoped had stops far beyond Newark. Within a few minutes, Marius was faced by a ticket collector. 'Can I have your ticket please sir?' proved to be one of the first English things said to Marius. This, for you to fully understand the experience, is the equivalent of being asked 'Ar turiu jūsu bilietas prašau ponas?' which I'm sure you don't understand. My computer certainly doesn't understand it and is reeling in grammatical shock. Marius looked at the ticket collector in a 'Please take pity, I'm from another country, and I've only been here five minutes and I can't speak English' sort of way. This succeeded in having no effect on the ticket collector apart from yielding an impatient look on his face. It was a small incident, but Marius was relieved when his father stepped in with 'He is wit mey. I have er tickets,' in English more broken than a former Tudor monastery, but English nevertheless.

However, this only puts off stating the fact that all arrived safely in Lincoln that night. Marius had forgotten all about his doubts concerning Lincoln's city status. If this place had been in Lithuania, thought Marius, it may have made it as the capital. It had so many things that were different from Lazdijai. The houses looked prettier and more charming, the roads were more organised and understandable, and the winter chill in the air was all the less bitter. 'So this is my life now,' thought Marius. But after so many miles, everyone agreed, they wanted a kip.

I am at St. John's School, Lincoln. A history classroom, to be precise. It has a high ceiling and desks that are peeling at the edges. I am sitting next to Marius, which I shall now concede is not his real name. He is 18, four years older than me; he has extremely short hair and quite wide eyes. I am nervous. This is an interview. And it is going badly.

For starters, I have spelt his name wrong. It is a *t,* not a *d.* It takes me some time to realise this. I am already stumped by his accent. In this small mistake and also in this forgettable session, lies the reason for the name change, in a tale that contains nothing that would get its main character arrested, deported, in court or murdered, if someone knew his identity. Firstly, I'm still not sure how to spell his name. Secondly, the interview went so horrifically wrong that I forgot to ask him any questions that were of any use or significance to the writing of this piece, therefore this is most likely to be not his story. The last reason is that if he came to read it, then he might not recognise that it is he who this is based upon. Nervously, I ask him what he feels is the biggest difference between Lithuania and his adopted home. 'The weather,' he says almost immediately. What did I expect? 'Worse?' I ask, thinking that I know his answer. 'No, better,' he says and then adds, 'in Lithuania you get much snow. It can be minus 20 in winter.' I am stunned. Minus 20! I am also informed that it doesn't rain as much in Lithuania. What a surprise. Later, Marius tells me how here opportunities and overall conditions are better. Both his parents work in a factory, but Marius says he lives in a house that is bigger than he could imagine. For certain, he is glad he no longer inhabits a stuffy, grey flat. I think I would agree. After this there is the longest of awkward pauses while my mind is blank – no questions or in fact anything useful to say. I notice that the teachers are looking at me, concerned. I rack my brain for something and then remember how two Polish teachers had briefed us beforehand. They had reminisced about how complex the British immigration process was. I decided to question Marius on this. 'So was it hard to get into Britain, then?' I enquire.

'No.'

Oh. Right then. It's not as if I wanted anything bad, cataclysmic or troublesome to happen to Marius and his family on their journey. It's just that I'm running out of ideas for this piece of writing I'm doing. I am also running out of questions on my short and hastily thought-out question list in my head. Silence once again descends on the misfiring conversation. Marius looks casually at his phone and then his timetable. 'So you made a lot of friends here, then?' I suddenly blurt out.

'Yeah' says Marius, cool as a cucumber on a Lithuanian winter's day.

'English friends too?'

'Yeah.'

'Did you know a lot of English before you came?'

'A bit'

'It's easier when you come to the country I suppose. To pick up the language.'

'Yeah.'

Actually I'm amazed at how good his English is. He has been in England for 15 months now, and apart from a few times when he says 'Say again,' he understands a whole range of things that I couldn't hope to understand in Lithuanian, even if I'd been learning it for four years. Actually…

'I've been learning German for over three years,' I say, pointlessly. 'Apparently I'm quite good, but I bet that I couldn't survive one minute if I actually went there.' Marius nods.

After a seemingly exaggerated amount of time, our time is finally up (yes, Yes, YES!). 'Is all that about me?' asks Marius, mildly surprised, mildly impressed. I hadn't thought it was enough.

It is only after I have walked out of the door of the classroom that I realise how fantastic the people who remain in it are. They have been on almost epic journeys, overcome the biggest of mental challenges and given up many things in their home country, just to come here. Dull, insignificant, wet, drab, boring old Blighty! For a better life, which they seemed to have achieved wonderfully. Despite all the problems they have had doing it, they are here. A country that they may not have heard much about before departing to live there. I can't even try to comprehend what they've been through. All I know is that they are immigrants and they are such amazing people.

John Freeman

Rožė

'I've missed you so much. When will I come and live with you?' asked Rožė.

Rožė, an only child, lived in Lithuania with her father. Her mother and father had split up when she was very young, and a year ago her mother moved to England. At this time, Rožė is talking to her mother over the phone. Recently it had been decided that she would move to England to live with her mum. She was scared – terrified in fact. She didn't know what to expect; all she had was the description of England from her mother. Apparently it was nice there, but what if her mother was wrong? What if Rožė hated England? There was no turning back once she got there.

That night Rožė sat in bed, bewildered. A million and one thoughts rushed through her head. It had been arranged that night for her to leave for England in two days time, apparently. The clock was ticking. She was thinking about what was to come and what she would be leaving behind. Her life in Lithuania wasn't bad, but it was definitely not good. She was poor and lived in a one-bedroom flat. The conditions were cramped and Rožė hated it. She climbed out of her bed and gazed out of the window. The grim, glum landscape that lay before her was her home. It wasn't heaven, but home is home after all. She studied the rows and rows of flats and the empty park, which during the day was full of bustling children. She could smell the freshly cut grass. Her hometown of Šilutė was small and contained only one park and three shops (two main supermarkets and a dress shop). Rožė loved the dress shop – she had bought a new dress from there just days before. It was a beautiful, bright blue, to match her eyes. She planned to wear it when she got to England. She wanted desperately to look nice for her mum. She didn't want to be an embarrassment to her mum, or for her mum to regret the decision and send her back.

The fatal day arrived. Rožė waited and waited all morning, listening to the droning sound of her teacher going on. Wanting, so badly, for the school bell to ring and for her dad to come and get her and take her to the airport. Then the big hand on the clock hit 12 and the little hand hit 1, and the sound and vibration of the bell ringing permeated her body. Her suitcase at hand, she forced her way past the crowd of children trying to get home and ran to the front door, giving it a hard shove. It flew open and there she saw her father waiting at the bottom of the steps for her. Her infectious smile covered her whole face. Yet her father looked far from happy, tears streaming down his face. Rožė could tell he was upset.

'Father, what's wrong?' she cried.

'Nothing sweetheart, I'm fine, I'm just going to miss you, that's all,' he replied, wiping the tears from his cheek and forcing a smile. She saw this as the perfect moment to give him a hug. She jumped up and swung her arms round him, the pair of them both laughing nervously.

Then it was time. The car pulled up to the airport in the centre of Šilutė. She looked up at the building. It was only small like the rest of the town, but had a lot of personal significance to Rožė. This would be the last building she would see in Lithuania. She heard a sudden roar and tilted her head back, looking up to see the plane coming in to land.

'Here it is,' her father said.

'What! That's my plane?' Rožė questioned.

'It is indeed. Nervous? Come on, let's get inside.'

She walked into the airport and went to check in her baggage. There was only a short queue so it didn't take her long, but it seemed like forever to Rožė as she was just anxious to board the plane. After checking in, she walked further through the airport to find her terminal. But there were still more obstacles stopping her from getting there. Security! This was a first for her. She'd never flown before and couldn't quite work out what the big archway and beeping batons were about. She walked towards them, under the archway and suddenly heard an echo of high-pitched beeps. What was happening? A man came towards her with the baton and waved it over her body; he then patted her shoulders, then her waist and worked his way down. Rožė was terrified – what was he doing? Why wasn't anybody stopping him? Her father laughed and told her not to worry. She suddenly felt OK then. She went past security and looked behind her to see her father waving frantically. She smiled and walked outside, and while she was waiting she counted the number of people boarding her plane with her. Ten!

She sat down in seat E5 and pulled out a box from her bag. The box was decorated with photos of her father and her friends. Inside the box were letters. She took the top one out and began to read.

Dear Rožė,

I am going to miss you. We're all going to miss you here. School won't be the same without you. You are, and always will be, my best friend. I can't believe you're leaving me. I hope you come back and visit. Don't ever forget me but make sure you don't dwell on it. Make new friends and enjoy your life in England and don't worry about me. I'm so happy for you; you're finally going to get what you always wanted, the chance to live with your mum. I love you. Best Friends.

Elena xxxxxxxxxx

Rožė's eye's started welling up. All of her close friends had written her letters and put them into a box for her. She thought for a moment about how lucky she was to have such good friends. She panicked. Why was she doing this? She was going to leave them behind. She tried desperately to stop the tears from streaming down her face, but no matter what, they kept on coming. She was so tired; she'd spent the whole day worrying and now it had finally caught up with her. Her eyes drifted shut and she slept. The plane took off and hours later she opened her eyes to her new home. She was here, and many different emotions were rushing through her head. Too late to go back now.

Yvette Balfe

Seasonal Adjustments

Winter was probably the biggest change that happened. My father has commonly mentioned that there is less excitement and fewer things to do through winter. I would have to agree. The British winter is famous for being a cold, wet miserable time, with very little snow to spice it up. Norway would, of course, not be the same without the heavy snow and thick ice that dominates the country at this time of year. I remember hearing from him that the first snow this winter had fallen in late September 2008 – around a metre of it in the lower mountains. By January 2009, the north of the country was recording temperatures of -33 ℃. with snow in the mountains easily exceeding 5 m. He even read of one place where a drift had caused the snow to become 18 m deep!

The house was situated on an island comprising mainly of a not particularly high mountain (by Norway's standards) at the end of the Sognefjord, meaning that he learned to ski by travelling cross-country over the small, rocky hills that sit behind my grandfather's house and separate it from the sea on the other side of the island. You would have thought that the cold would have kept them inside for most of the five or six months that this weather lasted, but upon my putting this to him he made it most clear that he disagreed. After all, they had to keep on with their daily life, and there is never much to do inside, he thought. I know him and his brother, my uncle, once entertained themselves by rolling cars down a ramp; however, the slow speed which the cars were reaching dissatisfied them, so the game was improved upon by fetching water and pouring it down the ramp. Due to the cold climate this water would then freeze instantly, improving the speed dramatically.

I would imagine that the most exciting time would have been going to school, although he always denies it, as to them it was normal. Due to the position of the island, Sula, in the group,

Solund, a road was not routed to the house until the late eighties; therefore they took the boat to school. Of course my grandparents never escorted them to school; from when he started school at the age of seven, my uncle would drive the small ten-horsepower motor boat to school in any weather. When my father started, around two years later, it was his job to lean out over the front of the boat, and smash the ice in front. They would travel in and out of the islands, at one point going out into the Atlantic and at another manoeuvring the boat through a small gap with barely ten centimetres on either side. All this to get them to a home-made jetty, on the land of a farmer who had kindly agreed to take the children in his tractor to the nearest stop for the school bus, several miles away from where they had started. And as I have said, this was done in all weathers, even when huge storms brought gigantic waves as the remnants of tropical hurricanes that had originated in the Caribbean. Naturally it would never be allowed now, due to health and safety, but they had always got through without incident.

School, my father has always said, was never as thought-out as it is now here in England. The science lessons had little in the way of experiments, and the teacher always performed the few that did happen. The PE lessons were more like break time. Especially in winter, the teacher would allow anyone who wished (mainly the boys), to go outside and coordinate his or her own games while the rest sat inside with the teacher, where it was warm. For sports day the children were not placed into teams of houses; instead they represented themselves, and the individual person would win the day. I have heard that my father won more than once for his year; however, my mother, in an attempt to maintain modesty, has always reminded me that, despite it being the largest group in the school, it was still only one class of 20, and this was the secondary school! However, it is something to remember.

Finally there were the summers: a time during which temperatures could peak at a boiling 25 ºC, and days which my father would spend in many exciting ways. When my father was young, my grandparents built their house on the place where it is now, and it was during this time my father took advantage of the building materials around him. Apparently he spent several hours with his brothers around the sand heap that was being used for the building work, combing it with magnets, in an attempt to gather as much iron ore out of it as possible. I have heard that it was quite a successful effort, as I believe that they managed to fill a rather large jar with the stuff. What they intended to do with it I don't know! When this wasn't possible, they would find other things to entertain themselves. Once, I heard they were found to have spent an entire afternoon jumping off the top floor of the family barn, to land on the hay, which was stored below.

The biggest event that occurred throughout Solund was the hill-climbing event, which happened every summer holiday. It was a competition where competitors would have to gain as many points as possible by climbing the different hills in the area. Each person would gain a trophy stating the number of points they had gained, and the winner would get a second, larger trophy.

He had few problems coming over: his English was reasonable, as it is on the curriculum from seven; however, many people believe that, 15 years later, he still has an obvious Norwegian accent, something which I have never noticed – but then he has said himself that his grammar is not as good as mine.

Despite this, I believe my father, although I doubt he would ever admit it, misses the lifestyle he had before. Living in Norway, my father grew up hoping to be a civilian ship's captain, a career that was pursued after he left school. After having done a year's national service in the navy, he worked for a few shipyards before going to Trondheim for a degree in naval engineering. He came over after several years of being pen-pals with my mother, and married her and now definitely considers himself British. However, when you live in a suburb of Lincoln, you rarely get to go out boating, there are few hills to climb and no prize if you do. And there are few barns which he would be permitted to jump from, if his physical ability allowed. And of course he hasn't skied since. I watch him and notice that he has deliberately limited his free time, possibly because of the few things he seems to be able to do with it. I can almost sense the melancholy boredom that he feels, that is his city life in England.

Kristian Lending

Imran

CRACK! There we were, the dirt and dust in our eyes, our mouths. I could not vouch for my friends but…

CRACK!… each time that bullwhip crashed onto my back it felt even more painful and I didn't know if I…

CRACK!… could stand it for much longer. All I wanted at that moment was for the ground to swallow me up…

CRACK!… I knew it would not happen yet. I prayed so hard that it would.

In Pakistan, drinking alcohol is frowned upon, and in some places definitely not allowed. In my small village, Doaba, in central Pakistan, strong Muslim convictions meant that drinking alcohol was out of the question.

I was a market trader in Doaba, just selling food to local people. Yet, once a month I, and three friends, would go to Kohat – a nearby large town – to buy produce to sell on in our village. On one trip we also acquired four bottles of beer, as drinking was frowned upon but not banned in Kohat. Due to our naivety, we took them back to our village and drank one bottle each. Big mistake!

People found out, and even now I don't know how. So, if the villagers found out then so did the law enforcers. At six o'clock they barged their way into my family's home and dragged me outside. They pushed and pulled me so that I lay on my stomach and they tied me down. We lay there for two hours with one of the law enforcers staring at us with a grim smile on his face. Occasionally he would glance around at people who were gathering to view what would become of us. Throughout those two hours we didn't say a word. I could not stop regretting drinking that beer. It wasn't even that nice.

As the crowd was becoming rather large – at least 250 – we knew that the thick hard leather bullwhip would be unleashed onto our bare backs. All I could do was question my decision. Was it really that bad? How would I cope after this? Would my parents

disown me? The time was fast approaching, the heat from the sun was scorching my back and the sunlight was near to blinding me. Then it came…
CRACK!

Isaac Liversidge

Escape

My first encounter with M took place in a Catholic church, and without speaking to him or his family, I gave it very little thought. I didn't stop to question what had brought him to this country, nor did I really have any reason to. It was not until I began to get to know one of his daughters that I discovered more about his life.

He had left his life in the Philippines, where he worked as a doctor and lived with his wife Melanie and their seven children, to come to London alone in 2002. His mother- and brother-in-law already lived in London, and told him that the country was crying out for more doctor's. Planning to test the waters, and then possibly be joined by his family, he left his homeland for England.

Previously, he had no real reason to leave. He ran a successful private doctors' surgery – there is no equivalent of the NHS in the Philippines – and his wife ran a textiles business that was worth 50 million pesos. Pesos are the Filipino currency, and M estimates that about 80 pesos are worth one pound sterling. They were cared for, and his was a well-off family.

Then the country's corrupt government, led by Ferdinand Marcos and his wife Imelda, was ousted by Cory Aquino in a peaceful revolution. In 1992 the economy failed drastically, and suddenly the family's money was worth a fraction of what it had been. Patients could no longer afford to visit M's surgery, and sales in Melanie's company plummeted. A new life in Britain suddenly seemed a much better option. His wife joined him after three years in 2005, then his children the following year.

On, arrival, however, M discovered that finding work was nowhere near that easy. It wasn't for lack of trying: he worked to get his PLAB – a qualification for foreign doctors to prove their competency and enable them to work in this country – while he held his tourist status for a year, but was still denied employment in his career. Even after applying for a working visa, he had little more success. He says that he was a victim of racism even from those inside the profession who are immigrants themselves. Bureaucracy and red tape also, he says, stopped him from working. He is now at an age where employers disregard him in favour of new medical graduates. It's a vicious circle, as the longer he spends out of his profession, the harder it becomes for him to find a job.

When M relocated to Grantham, he had to work in Padleys, a food manufacturer, his skills going to waste. He found that while he worked hard, taking overtime when it was offered, many others were not working but were living on benefits. This gave him, and other immigrants to this country, a bad reputation by association. He found that he was subjected to unfairness and contempt, despite working legitimately and paying taxes.

It was hard to acclimatise to life in England. Racism was not something M had really come across before, yet suddenly it was a huge problem; a barrier preventing him from living as he wanted. After moving to Grantham, M says, the problem was worse: London is so culturally diverse that to be racist would be impossible or ill-advised. In Grantham, a small town where most of the inhabitants are white British, it is far more widespread. On the estate where he lives, a gang are often on his street, taunting his family and shouting abuse. Yet what gives them more of a right to live here, when M has worked harder than them but is denied job prospects?

His children met this difficulty, too. At their first school they were subjected to such hideous racism and bullying that they had to move, while at their next school they found life easier, but still came across discrimination from some. It seems grossly unfair that this family – who are living perfectly legitimately in this country – are seen only as part as an ethnic group. The children I know are intelligent and kind, and the family all seem respectful, well-behaved and generous; more so than many British people I have met who assume it is their 'right' to live here and enjoy the privileges so unfairly denied to M.

It was hard, also, to be away from his family. In the Philippines, extended families are close and family life is far more important than it is here. He has little time to spend with his large immediate family, either, because he often works overtime to provide for them.

Culture here is hugely different in other ways, too. In M's homeland, religion is important and much more widespread. In the region of the country that he comes from, the Spanish influence from the 13th to the 17th century means that 90% of the population is devoutly Roman Catholic. M believes that the lack of religion is largely to blame for our large crime figures. Religion, he says, is a reason to do 'good'. Without religion, conscience alone is clearly not strong enough, as there are still regular violent assaults. Back home, M says that while crime of course occurs, it is much less frequent, and less serious. Crime consists largely of petty theft and rarely, if ever, is there an incidence of violent crime. Here, only the most shocking serial murderers make the news. This is why M tries so hard to impress religion and the morality that it brings on his children. Aside from church every Sunday, the family attend prayer meetings with other Catholics.

There is also, M says, a culture of promiscuity at an early age in the UK. This could also be due to the lack of religious direction. Teenage pregnancy figures are undeniably high, and M says he was shocked at how young his children were when they were taught sex education in school in this country.

His life took another turn for the worse after the July 2005 London bombings. Suddenly he found that many people saw him as a potential terrorist, just because of his race. Although the bombs are in the relatively distant past now, at the time many immigrants to this country said that they could clear a bus simply by getting on and opening a bag.

Life here isn't all bad news, though. M is keen to add that he has met true friends here who are honest and decent. This country offered his family an escape from their country when they needed it. Also, M says that he has found that people in Britain mean what they say. Whereas many Filipinos are shy and hide their feelings, the English seem to show others their emotions – surprising, as it is so contrary to the traditional view of the British repressing all emotions with their 'stiff upper lip'. This means that here, if someone falls out with you, they are friendly again the following day. In the Philippines, if somebody tells you that they are angry with you, then you are ill-advised ever to speak to them again. It's a very permanent thing.

Overall, however, though the family is perhaps richer in this country, life is not better. M has already decided that he plans to leave for the Philippines in a few years. The country is in a better state now, and he misses the ways of his homeland. This country doesn't seem like a good place to be at the moment. He says that he, his wife and some of the younger children will probably return in the not-too-distant future. Some of the older children, however, have grown up in this country and have grown accustomed to the culture and lifestyle. They may wish to stay here. Having been educated in Britain, they may have better prospects. The eldest children are old enough to make their own decisions about their future now. M feels that they may be 'between cultures', not really fitting in either.

While on the surface, it appears that our country offers a home to immigrants who need a new life, when you look more closely it is far more complicated. If, and when, M and his family leave to return to the Philippines, many people who have always lived in Britain will not realise that they have lost some people who have given more to us than we think. They have worked harder and been kinder than many British people. I don't wish to give the false impression that we are a nation of evil, racist people, but this country has not given M very much at all. While I hate to admit it, having found out more about their lives, it seems that M and his family are right to think that they will have a better life back home in the Philippines. They will at least be away from the hidden side of this nation that we all seem to be so proud of – the nation that had always seemed to me to be so beautiful – but which can be ugly indeed.

Fiona Kelk

Andrzej

'Don't do it!' my mother begged. But I had to. We had to. I was 15. Everyone was terrified. We lived in fear of the German attack, night after night thinking deeply about what may happen, and thinking the worst. And the worst happened. The border between Germany and Poland became a war zone. Horror struck the land, all of the flowers died and somehow the brightness in the sun and the happiness in the birds' song disappeared. The Germans stormed through, killing our people and taking control of our land. Our people and our land. They took everything, our homes, our friends and our loved ones. Children cried out, louder and louder. Women fell to their knees, their husbands lying dead, motionless before them. The sounds of guns and screams of pain rattled through the once busy, adored streets of our country.

Before the terror arrived I lied to the authorities and told the Polish army that along with my friends I too was 17, and was ready to fight for my country. As I stepped out of the front door of our tiny family house I realised that this was it. I was going to war. Going to kill. My mother cried and hugged me so tight it was as though she would never see me again. 'I will be fine,' I lied. I knew that the Germans were strong and thirsty for victory, and so did she. I felt alone and vulnerable, and I was. Walking away that day I never looked back. I could not bear to.

When the attack came, I did not know what to do with myself. I killed men. Men whose families were at home, living in hope of their return. I destroyed the lives of others. Was I a murderer? I began to lead a different life; I was not myself any longer. How could I be?

Now it was my turn. The feeling that I felt is indescribable. My arm, the pain, I could hear men shouting and the sound of guns rumbling, but somehow I was distant from that. I felt like a small boy again, except this time there was no one to help me, no one to comfort me and tell me that I will be OK. After a while I came to and realised that I had been shot in my left arm. Yes the pain was bad, but more than that the fact that this had happened to me left me in shock, me. Just weeks ago I had been at home with my family. I had been a child; I had no worries and felt safe. My life changed in the firing of a gun. I had to leave. I could not do this.

I arrived in Scotland with nowhere to go, penniless and alone. To me, though, anything was better than what I had come from. I took a breath of fresh air and somehow felt safe. But I never stopped thinking. My school friends, my idols and my enemies were dying. They were living in constant torment and terror, everyday they woke not knowing if they would ever wake up again, if they would ever hold their loved ones again, if they would ever achieve their dreams of becoming doctors, dentists, and most importantly, free men. I prayed every night for every single one of those men, our own and the enemy. Despite the vivid and passionate hatred I felt for Germany, those men were doing their duty, they had hopes and dreams like me, and they did not deserve to die.

I went from place to place for a while. Looking back on it, I was just a young boy. I must have been just 17 when I met and married my wife. We had a small wedding in Edinburgh, just us. I could not have wanted more. I had found love and companionship. Someone to heal the holes that the war had left me with.

I wanted to provide for my family, to give them a happy life, to give them the security of a stable and loving home. 'We will survive,' my wife told me, 'as long as we have each other, we will be fine.' There was no work for me in Scotland and it was hard because I was Polish and still a young man with little experience. So we moved down south to Lincoln where my wife, Jane, had family.

We settled here. I eventually found a job at a garage, as a petrol pump assistant. I became fascinated by cars, and taught myself a trade. I watched the men working on cars day after day, intently, and eventually bought my own garage. I felt proud of what I had made of myself, and the business was successful. It remains in the family to this day.

After the war, Russia took over Poland and communism was introduced to the country. I knew little of what went on at home, only what I heard on the radio. The first time I went back was in 1966. The first 50 miles of land was no-man's-land, it was unclaimed and was a home to the Russian Cossacks. They were extremely poor, and I felt a wave of thankfulness as I watched them from the window of the taxi. As I got further into the country, I noticed how much communism was influencing the way people lived.

Arriving home brought back memories of the day I had left. My mother was an elderly woman now; she hardly recognised me and when I explained that it was me, she hugged me like before, but this time she cried 'He is alive, my baby, he is alive!' Tears filled her eyes and she told me that she had always had faith. I met my sister for the very first time. She was 23 years old and I had never even known that she had existed. I learned that my family was only safe and protected because Lenka (my sister) had married a man who was in the communist party. Unlike many others, my family had been extremely lucky. I felt as though my prayers had been answered.

Although I loved my family and my country very much, I did not want to move back. I had made my life in England now and I was happy and content with it. However, I will always remember the men who died, the men who fought hard and brave. I just have to hope that somewhere, there are men with stories like mine. Men who were able to see the sheer joy in their families' eyes when they came home. Men who were able to achieve their dreams and live long and happy lives. Men who had been blessed.

Penny Miller

Nerves and Preconceptions

Nerves. That was the only thing I felt. Part of me just wanted to get back on the bus and go back to my school. Somewhere where I felt safe. I was like a fish out of water, in a different school, and about to meet a complete stranger and delve straight into her life. What if she didn't like me? What if I didn't like her? What if she thought I was rude and just walked out? I didn't know what to expect.

I felt guilty after a while, making all of these assumptions. Maybe she might be thinking the same things. So I decided to get a grip and just go and meet the girl. How bad could it be? That was the point where I realised how selfish I was being. Just thinking about myself and how this meeting would affect me, not even considering the feelings of the person I was about to meet and me just waltzing in there and expecting her to pour out her life story just so I can have something to write about. It was a selfishness that I would later come to regret.

I walked into the classroom looking round for the person I was supposed to be interviewing but the only people there were a few teachers. Confusing. We were then taken to another classroom where I met Dominica. Dominica Nowak. Dominica was born on the 7th July, and is an 18-year-old girl from Zielona Góra, a city in Lower Silesia in Western Poland. She moved to England two years ago. She and her mother had come on holiday and never gone back.

I thought that she would be full of praise for Lincoln, listing endless things that are better here than in her home town. Oh how mistaken I was. She hates it here. Hates it. I'm going to be honest; I was shocked when she first said she wished she had never moved here, shocked and somewhat resentful towards her. How dare she? She should be grateful to live in such a lovely, safe environment. But she wants to go back to Poland. Dominica says she hates the fact that Polish people move here and we shouldn't be living in other people's countries.

She then went on to explain. She told me how hard it was living here, not being able to just have a simple conversation with someone. She said she dreaded it if her mum asked her to go to the shops, because she knew that it would be awkward and uncomfortable if she said something wrong or got her words mixed up. Even though she learned English at school back in Poland, she says she really only knows enough to be able to survive here and knows how to ask for the hospital and other important services. I thought she was being rather hard on herself, I thought her English was just fine. I was able to talk to her and understand, her but as we progressed in the interview I began to see what she meant as she stopped occasionally to get her pocket-sized dictionary out and look up a word and show me.

I then asked her why else she didn't like this country. She said she didn't feel welcome. People at her school and near where she lives judge her because she is Polish. That feeling of resentment that I felt when she said she hated it here just went flying out the window. I felt ashamed and embarrassed at the fact people like me, of my nationality, would be so horrible and unkind towards someone in somewhere so alien and so far from home. We should be trying to help her feel welcome, not beating her up at any opportunity. Dominica went on to describe how some days she just feels like not getting up.

I asked why she chose to move here. Dominica said that her mother wanted to get away for a while after she and her father had split up. She said her mum only stayed here because she wanted a better life for Dominica. She says her mum has more money over here but she works all the time, and Dominica only sees her for about three hours every day. I asked her if she missed her father.

'No,' she said.

Again I jumped to conclusions, wondering how she could be so blunt about one of the people who had brought her into the world. She said she misses him occasionally because, after all, he is her father. She looked as if she was about to burst into tears. My mind was whizzing around, trying to find something to say to change the subject. But she told me anyway. She said he drank; he was an alcoholic. I found out he had turned to alcohol after enduring an accident in the mines in which he had lost one of his legs. I was stunned. I didn't know what to say. How does she do it? To be so frighteningly honest with a complete stranger.

It was at that moment that I felt truly disgusted with myself; looking back at earlier in the day when I was just thinking about myself and there she was, just sat pouring her life out to me. I had grown to admire her. All of the stuff she'd been through in her life and she still got on with things; everything she has to deal with and worry about like getting just a bit of money to get from one day to the next. And then there's me, who worries what my hair looks like and gets annoyed if my mum doesn't buy me everything I want.

At the end of the interview, I didn't think of her as just a girl from a different country I interviewed once; I came to think of her as a friend, someone I admired for her strength and will. I keep in touch with her and we still speak to the very moment I am writing this. I truly believe that Dominica is an inspiration and it really did open my eyes to the stereotypes that we people in Britain put on Polish people that move here for a better life.

Rosy Broughton

Krzysztof

'Today, everybody, we are welcoming a new member into our class. His name is Krzysztof and he is from Poland.' The young Polish boy stared at all the English faces gazing up at him. Some children at the back of the class sniggered. Even though he could not understand them yet, Krzysztof knew that it wasn't going to be easy to settle into such a different way of life.

'Why does school start so early in England?' This was one of the many questions about this new place that he had. His mum had explained that it would take a while for him to pick up the language and the differences, but going to a school where he could surround himself with all these things could be the thing that helped him carry on as normal. His older sister, Anastazja, was finding it easy to settle into the mood of things but it was harder for him. When you are that age, it is a crucial time, when you most need the security of friendship and a continuous net of regulation and safety to keep the naivety and innocence that comes with still only being a child.

'But Mum, why do we have to leave? I have so many friends here and so do you and Dad,' Krzysztof used to complain before they left their homeland.

'Because your dad and I think it is for the best, Krzysztof, and there is nothing you can say that will change our minds.' As much as he tried, his mum was right: there was nothing at all that could change their minds about the move.

This was just the beginning of the story. I met Krzysztof a year later and it seems that he is still adjusting to life here in England. He sat on the end of the table avoiding people's gaze and fidgeting; I could tell he was nervous. Although he had only been living in the country for just over a year, and (as I later found out) did not speak any English when he first arrived, he understood the majority of my questions and managed to reply with only a few interventions from the teacher. I was amazed at how a boy who was three years younger than me managed to come to a foreign country and learn the ways of life here; I don't think I would have been able to manage. Their new house is near the centre of town, with a much smaller living space and smaller garden. When I asked Krzysztof about the differences between life here and life in Poland, I saw him well up with the memory of his simple life from before. I realised that this was a sensitive subject and decided that any other questions about his old life would have to be phrased carefully.

'Can I go out to play with Borys this evening?'

'Sorry, not tonight darling.'

'It's not fair! I never go out with my friends!' This was one of the problems with England, thought Krzysztof. Mum and Dad don't let me go out any more. They knew everyone in the town of Trzebunia, south of Kraków. Being in England meant that they were more cautious and couldn't trust people because they didn't know them. They should be grateful I have friends, thought Krzysztof. Life hadn't always been a barrel of laughs. When they first arrived, it was hard. Not knowing the language put a large barrier between Krzysztof and his peers. People made fun of him because of his nationality and even though he couldn't understand them word for word, bullying is easy to recognise in any language.

'You understand, don't you Puss.' Although this was not the same cat that they had back in Poland, she was still a great comfort to him. She would sit on his lap and listen to all his worries about England and then go off hunting. If it had been a particularly bad day then she would bring back a present for Krzysztof. I asked if he spoke to the cat in Polish or English and he replied 'a bit of both'. I had never met a multi lingual cat before, and I wasn't sure if anyone else had either.

'Have you been back to Poland?'

'Yes.'

'Do you miss it?'

'Yes.' Getting answers from this little boy was going to be hard work, I could tell.

After a few awkward pauses I asked, 'So, what do you want to do when you grow up?'

'I want to move back to Poland and be a driver like my father.' This was a very definite answer; it was clear that he had made up his mind a while ago. Even though he now understood the decision that his parents had made a year ago, he obviously still disagreed with them. In a couple of years maybe his plans will change, and he will decide that perhaps staying in England would be a good thing. Maybe he would never be completely satisfied with English life; there would always be that connection with Poland.

Hannah Faulkner

Ewa

What do you remember about The nineties? Iconic music, unique fashion, perhaps some more personal memories of your own past. But you probably don't remember the 2nd February 1991, in Poland, and the birth of Ewa Dudek.

No reason to, right? Never even heard of her. But she's not just something to dismiss so easily. Ewa is 18 years old, a complex bundle of chemicals and emotions centred on a human soul. Immense potential and infinite possibility, all contained in a package entirely unique, and so instantly breathtaking that it's intimidating for me to even sit opposite her.

Maybe she senses it. She smiles. It's awkward.

'Hi.'

'Hi,' I reply lamely, equally embarrassed.

She glances at her friends, and I glance at mine. We're all looking to each other for help, not entirely sure what this interview is meant to entail, silently asking for one of us to take charge. No one wants to intrude so brutishly. I sigh, and turn back to the girl across from me, flash her a smile, and put forward the only thing I can think of to start with.

'So… what's your name?'

'Ewa,' she tells me, relief filling her prettily accented tone. 'What is yours?'

I smile uselessly as my name escapes me. 'Um,' I provide helpfully.

She blinks.

I laugh for a second, mostly out of nerves, and then my mind alights on the word I'm looking for.

'Laura.'

'Laura? That's pretty.'

'Thank you,' I mumble. I examine my shoes.

It's not an amazing start.

Gifted and Talented. That's me, apparently, and a few far more deserving friends of mine, and that's why we're on a trip to this school. They want us to write a piece on heritage, or more specifically, on heritages different to our own. So we've been paired up with random students who fit the description, strangers, and allowed out of our own school to visit theirs.

It's certainly a different experience. I find later it's something my friends were nervous about, dreading for days the idea of parading down corridors in pristine blazers and ties, deliberately defying their instincts and drawing hostile attention to themselves. We would be *the posh kids*.

I don't realise this until I'm actually in the school. My friends huddle in a close group and peer around nervously. One or two have pulled coats on in an attempt to hide the defining uniform, have tried everything to make their appearance look neutral. Sadly, I've had no such forethought, standing out a mile in dark make-up, a choker, chain, fingerless gloves that all scream *stereotype*. At least following me, my friends look normal. I don't mind. The comments are pretty spiteful.

It's not until the atmosphere has relaxed and we're a few minutes into the interview that Ewa chooses to touch on the subject of my unusual appearance, and only because she's prompted to do so by the girl who walks past and hisses an insult.

'I'm sorry,' she says immediately, glaring after her.

'I get it a lot,' I answer dryly.

'Me too,' she answers sympathetically, turning her attention back to me. I'm confused.

'You do?'

She's entirely stunning, dressed conservatively enough, and she half-smiles uneasily as I realise what she must be referring to.

'What? They're racist?'

She twists her mouth, as though she doesn't want to condemn people with the word, and shrugs. Her friends and mine have both fallen silent and are watching us, and her eyes flick over to them. I'm suddenly struck by the realisation of how sheltered I am, how naive.

'Us three,' she says, and frowns while she searches for a word.

'We stick,' her friend provides, and they nod and say

simultaneously, 'We stick together.'

'Because they don't like you?' I ask, tactless in my disbelief.

'The boys, they will talk to us. The girls, no. No. They don't like us.'

I force a smile to disguise my shame at being English.

'Maybe it's because you're all gorgeous.'

Ewa blushes, and she thanks me as they dissolve into giggles.

I laugh with her. I pity the ones that won't let themselves.

Ewa and her family moved over to England three years ago, when she was just 15. She explains this to me vividly, talking more excitably and comfortably now, throwing in the odd Polish word. I refuse to point out I can't understand. I admit to her I know nothing of world geography, ask her a little about her country of origin. We experience a block.

'What currency does Poland have?' I query, staring down at my notes. I look up to see her staring worriedly at me.

'Er... I...'

I don't want to be so obtuse as to just repeat something more slowly and loudly. I cycle through synonyms mentally and spend a moment cursing my seemingly pretentious vocabulary. My friends have trouble understanding me at times, let alone someone who claims she's terrible at English.

'What... um.'

I turn to my friends, and they seem to sympathise, to chew on their lips as they try and help me substitute a word.

Ewa is looking at hers too, conferring low and fast before she turns to me.

'I don't understand.'

I can't help but grin. She says it slowly, but with an undertone of pride – she's glad she can communicate with me. I immediately feel like learning Polish for her. I'd dedicate years of study to make this girl comfortable.

'What money do you use?' I explain, and my friend chips in.

'Like, pounds. Or euros.'

'Oh! Curr – Currency?' She tries the word out, and we nod.

She pulls out a sheet of paper and a pen, scrawls down what I can assume is the Polish equivalent before asking me stiltedly:

'How you spell…?'

I spell it for her in fascination as she writes it down, another word added to her impromptu dictionary of the day. I've already forgotten about getting an answer as I begin to throw more questions out.

'You have language classes, right? Is this what you do?'

'Language classes, yeah. We write things they don't teach us here.'

She taps the paper with the pen. I lean forward.

'May I?'

She offers it over to me and I unfold it, skim quickly down the list. To me, there seems to be a plethora of new words for everyday use.

'That's a lot,' I comment redundantly.

'I'm bad at English.'

She accepts the sheet back with a self-deprecating smile as I try and follow the implications of the two-sentence exchange. It seems as though she feels it's her fault there's a lot to learn.

'You seem fluent to me,' I observe in confusion. I can only assume her modesty is at play.

'Thank you!'

She beams. I beam.

We're fluent with each other *that* way.

'So, how often do you have language classes?'

I'm restraining myself from firing a barrage of questions at her. There's a lot I want to ask, but I figure it's her turn to throw a few back at me soon. It's a shame I'm nowhere near as interesting.

'Every day,' she tells me. 'Two hours.'

'Do you get homework?'

'Yes… sheets. Fill in words.'

'Difficult?'

'For me, yes! Her, not so much.'

She gestures to the girl on her left and they share a grin. She looks at me again.

'Do you learn language?'

'German. I'm pretty bad.'

She nods, empathetically. 'It's hard!'

I have a German oral scheduled in a week. I immediately stop worrying over it and try to imagine I had to learn a language entirely, not just vocabulary that might be useful to me. And not just for a school test, but for the foundation of my everyday life. The total frustration of not being able to express myself, having to stumble over new words and hope they might be close enough. I'd worry I was losing my heritage. I'd worry I was losing myself.

'What do you want to be?' I ask childishly, on impulse. I want to put her back in control. I want her to define herself in ways she loves.

'I want to work in travel,' she tells me excitedly. 'I love geography. A travel agent. Give people holidays. Absorb… culture. Go around the world.'

I smile.

'I want to… show myself, in all traditions,' she elaborates. 'Meet people. Respect customs. Learn history. Discover. Adventure!'

My teacher taps me on the shoulder. It's time to leave. I rise out of my seat, and so does she.

'Ewa?'

'Mmm?'

'How do you say thank you in Polish?'

She hugs me.

Laura Smith

Their Own World

I was standing in the airport, waving goodbye to my family, wondering whether they would return. Whilst I was in the place I had known and lived in all my life, my sister Alina felt apprehensive as to what experiences and emotions the unknown city of London would bring her.

After she'd spent a few days settling in at their new home I received a phone call from my sister. She was quieter than normal. Lack of sleep often made her grumpy and perhaps it was the busy settling-in period that had made her like that. Alina said it was strange not having our grandparents living literally next door. Living with Mum's friend was quite cramped, but it was interesting to have someone we knew to support us with English life. It must have been strange, not really ever feeling at 'home' for a while. But I knew how she felt.

Soon after, my brother and I joined our family in London. This was when I understood for myself what it was like to move away from home, just like Alina had done a few weeks earlier. Our house in Poland was huge and the family could fit comfortably in it. Due to our family living so close by, there was no need for us to travel around much, so moving about one thousand miles was very abnormal. In Kielce there wasn't much to do. Lack of shops and buildings made it monotonous and not much happened from day to day. You'd have thought that every person was your friend; you were unable to pass someone without greeting him or her or making a friendly gesture.

But London was a different picture altogether. The streets were full of people in their own world. It was the opposite of Kielce; people were always talking to other people on their phones instead of actual face-to-face human interaction. Surrounding the busy city there seemed to be a big, thick smog cloud that added to the trapped feeling I got when walking down the cramped streets. The good thing about London for Mum and Alina was the variety of clothing shops. The money-spending brought back memories of Alina's days out with her friends in Poland. I know that one of the things she preferred in London was the shopping. I guess, memories of Poland just made Alina miss home more. It was not about the past. It was about the future: a better standard of living, new friends and a new home.

One aspect of this new life my family and I were approaching was school. I was starting Year 11. Alina and I were making our trek to school. Well, it was a couple of miles but it felt like ages compared to the small journey we had back in Kielce. Although I've only been here for a few days, I have already found myself comparing everything to my old home. Our new school was one big difference. As Alina and I went through the daunting school gates I could feel dubious eyes fixed on us. It was so unusual for them to have someone new. Alina had started subconsciously biting her lip like she always has done when she gets embarrassed. Finally we had passed and began to make our way to the headteacher's office. The stunned silence from the other students faded and it reverted back to the usual hustle and bustle you would expect at school.

As we proceeded to the head's room we were met by a huge, closed door. We had found it. I stood tall whereas Alina had already concealed herself behind me. I wasn't short for my age but against this door I felt like an ant. I went to knock, when the door was flung open and answered by a man. The Head of the school had met us; he was a tall and content looking man and I felt a little less anxious after meeting him.

Alina and I had now been split into our separate years and forms. We had met up at lunchtime to talk about how our day had panned out so far. Whilst I was quite happy and thought I was settling in OK, Alina was quite different.

For her it had been a long morning. She had sat on her own most lessons, and the other girls were talking about things she was not very familiar with. Mum and Dad had expected me to be the one that had not settled as well, but Alina – she just burst into tears. 'I hate it here! Please can we go home?' she snivelled. Our parents tried to comfort her but I think it was something she was going to have to get over and sort for herself.

After a prolonged unpacking period the house was finally furnished and felt cosier. An early night's sleep was what we all needed after the chaos and commotion the past few days had brought us. I felt reasonably confident that London wasn't going to be as bad as first thought. I was just worried as to how Alina was going to get on tomorrow.

I awoke to silence, which was odd because my sleep is normally interrupted by Alina blasting the hairdryer, preening herself like every teenage girl does. But I was the first one up this morning; Dad wasn't starting work until next week and, well, Alina wasn't around. I ran into her room, ready to jump onto her bed in an attempt to wake her up and start our usual brotherly, sisterly banter, when out of the corner of my eye I spotted something. A small piece of paper with Alina's writing. I read it, having to take a second look to realise what it really meant: 'I need to sort things out with this new place on my own for a while, Love Al x.'

I ran into my parents. They were sat up watching the TV, no idea of what I had just discovered. They read through the note and immediately grabbed the phone to get in contact with Alina. All they got was voicemail.

Olivia Hendry

Being Accepted

I approached her feeling cowardly. At this point I didn't know her name, and to be honest I didn't really want to. She didn't seem like the kind of person who I would want to get to know. We sat facing each other, barely looking at each other. This anticipation continued for quite a while. 'Hi?' I eventually said. She looked up, and replied, 'Emm... hi...' This sort of conversation went on for a while, you know the small talk, hi, and how are you, and so on and so on. The kind you would have with your grandma, the boring sort. It was about time we actually started talking about what I had gone for.

She began to tell me the story of how she ended up in Lincoln.

Goodbye

'Goodbye, Goodbye!' is all I could hear as we walked towards the plane. I looked up at my mum standing next to me. She stopped. She looked back at Alexsander and simply smiled, nothing else, just smiled and turned back to her original direction. The closer we got to the plane the more my hope and desire increased, hope and desire for that better life that so many people deserve. I turned to my mum – 'Will I ever see Alexsander again?' She looked down at me and placed her hand on my cheek. It was at this point I felt her fear. 'We will see!' she said to me. My heart sank, the thought of not ever seeing him again, my own brother, it was horrible.

The next morning I awoke, slowly and anxiously, trying to anticipate what I would see. A sigh of relief. We had arrived at our new home. Well at least that's what Mum called it; it just didn't feel like that to me. It was Grandma's house; she said we could stay there, while Mum saved some money. I hated it; we used to live in such a big house, and now this, a small, claustrophobic terraced house. I stood at the window of the room Mum said was mine. I looked out at the view, well there wasn't really much of a view. I saw more houses like the one I was in, and then a small shop on the corner to my left. At the end of the street was another road. It was very busy... a lot more busy than in Kielce. That is all I could do, compare. I couldn't help myself – everything that I saw, I compared with Kielce.

The High Street

I remember, after we settled down, Grandma said we should go shopping, to see Lincoln, see what it's like and what there is. So we did. As we left the house, I noticed our neighbour was going into his house. He didn't even smile. This shocked me; I was so used to growing up in a close, friendly atmosphere and overnight I was living here. The busy road I mentioned earlier, that was the high street. We started walking down it. We were meant to be going shopping but, because I didn't know any of the shops, I wasn't really interested.

This gave me a chance to start to get used to the area and the people who live here. It was hard for me to take anything in. Even though I have studied English since primary school in Poland, it was so different, and I couldn't really understand a thing. Not being able to speak English was a really big shock. I knew now that there was a lot for me to get used to. Everybody was very, erm... individual. I noticed that there was very little communication between the different people. It was different from Poland – pretty much everyone spoke to everyone in Poland: it was a way of life, it was just how things were there. This kind of atmosphere was very different, it was so different that I often felt awkward or out of place – an outsider. I didn't feel welcome like I thought I would.

Settled Down

Time has moved on now, it is a few months since we first moved to England. We got our own house a few streets away from Grandma. It's a little bit smaller than Grandma's, but it's only Mum and me living here. It's great; Mum deciding to come here was the best decision she has ever made. Life is so different from how it used to be, but better though – a lot better. I have lots of friends now, I spend a lot of time with them and I don't have to worry about Mum being on her own because she has made friends at work too, and some friends from Poland live here as well. My friends are great – they are so friendly and they teach me so much, especially the English ones; oh and I have a few Polish friends too! It is better me having a mix of friends, that way I can learn new things but at the same time have someone who I can talk to properly.

School

As most of my friends are at school they help me a lot, with understanding and learning. Speaking of school, wow, now that is something worth telling you about. Sometimes it's so different but so often it reminds me of back in Poland. The best thing about school here in England is that there is always someone to help me; I am never left on my own. We have this teacher, who is Polish herself, who helps a group of people who have, like me, come to England. She is great and helps us in lessons and sits with us when we have exams. The school itself is very good as well, the whole atmosphere is very friendly, and I often feel like everybody wanted to be everybody's friends – a lot different to what it was like on the high street. Must be just the older people who are mardy!

Although I love the school here in England, it just doesn't feel like Poland. I don't know why but I much prefer my old school. It could be just because the work is different, but I really don't know. I suppose I feel like this about a lot of stuff; everything here in England is great but nothing compares to Kielce, my home, my real home. But then, I wouldn't want to go back either. I know, I know, I don't make much sense… let me try and explain. I love Poland – it's my home – but moving to England was a really difficult thing for me to do, leaving my friends and having to start afresh and having to do all of that again isn't worth me leaving what me and Mum have built up here in England, and anyway we are happy, so why would we want to ruin that?

The News For Alexsander

Nine months ago today we moved into our own house and both my Mum and me are happy. Last night we got a Chinese takeaway. I had no idea why, Mum usually makes something, but I know now: it was a celebration – Mum had some news for me. She has been saving since we moved into our new house, and now she thinks she has enough money to pay for Alexsander to come to England. It's just brilliant, I have missed him so much. Well to be honest, over time I have got used to him not being here, but when Mum told me this I just wanted to see him so much, more and more every second. Mum wanted me to write him a letter to let him know that we had organised everything, so, I did.

Alexsander

I have missed you so badly; I am sorry that we have not talked for such a long time and I really hope everything in Polska is going well. Mum told me that you passed your test – WELL DONE!!!!

You may be able to tell from this letter that I am picking up English very well. It is a real challenge but I'm getting there. The school I am at is great, other than a few people, but I try my best to ignore them.

Life here in England. is not much different. I love Lincoln but it is huge compared to Kielce. There are so many shops and Mum and me love to go shopping. I even bought you something.

I also have some great news for you. Mum was going to tell you but I needed to be the one who told you. Mum told me yesterday that we now have enough money to pay for you to come to England. That is, if you want to. Mum said you might not, but you can come if you want to. If you do decide you want to come and live in England then you need to let us know.

Hopefully you'll be with us for Christmas next year:-D - (a smile face Rachel taught me). I will try and keep you updated, but will see you soon.

We all love you so so so much here in England.

Alina xxx

I was so exciting writing this letter. It meant so much to me being able to tell my brother this. For me to give him this opportunity; well not just him, but the whole family. This is the final stage of our plans; it would be the cherry on the cake.

The End

I cannot believe it; Alexsander came back yesterday, and it's November. He is back in time for Christmas. He has been back for a day now and it feels like he has been here for ages. It's a great feeling, the whole family together again, but this time better than before – this time we are happy. Instead of some of us being happy when the others are feeling down… now we can all share the happiness.

I cannot believe the difference in my life, our family being given this opportunity is simply amazing. I feel that everybody should be given this opportunity. Why can't they? Many people just don't accept the fact that people only go to other countries because they need a better life. They get to the stage where they physically cannot cope with the life they are living so they decide to move, much like I did. But more often than not, they are not accepted by the location they move to and end up having to move again. Often, when they move, it is out of necessity, not choice.

This thankfully isn't me. I moved but I was accepted. My family is happy, and grateful.

Liam Moat

Her Life

What is it that makes someone leave their home country? What drives them to leave everything behind? They lose their friends, family and home with all its memories. But lots of people do leave. We see them every day, just passing us on the street. Most of us merely think to ourselves, 'Oh, it's just yet another immigrant, here to work,' and we ignore them. Some people may even disapprove of these people, giving them dirty looks as they walk by. We rarely stop to think that each individual person has a story to tell. A story of what made them come here and leave everything they knew behind. A story, perhaps of struggle, or maybe simply a wish come true. A story that has changed their lives forever. Here is just one woman's story, of why she came all the way from Poland to England, and ended up working in the Grantham branch of Lloyds TSB.

New Start

A new job! Finally! Katarzyna was ecstatic. At last, something to be proud of; something to celebrate. It was a chance in a million that she should be given this opportunity and she still couldn't believe it. How did she progress from a small, insignificant child in a tiny Polish village, to a quality controller in a small, stuffy vegetable factory near Boston, and then all the way to working in one of the best and most trusted banks in England? Simply because she helped out a friend. A friend who couldn't speak English and who needed to open a bank account. And Katarzyna was offered a job! Just because she could speak good English, according to the person who worked there. She gave her details to the employee, but, to be honest, expected no reply. You can imagine her surprise when, a few days later, she received a phone call asking her to come down for an interview. The interview went fairly well, but she still didn't expect anything more, and then, suddenly, a few days after that she was offered the job! A new, and much better one in the Boston branch of Lloyds TSB. After all her effort and toil, she finally has an occupation that reflects her hard work.

With this chance, she can complete what she came to England to do in the first place – pay her parents back. They had spent a huge amount of money on her and her education and she decided it was time to repay them, especially since they had always supported her decisions too. And now she can. She no longer wanted to be dependent on them; no longer wanted to take their money. After all, there were her brothers to consider too; her parents couldn't just spend their money on her. So she came here to earn for herself, which had been a bit of a disaster up until now. But now she has a job that she can enjoy, her life will be different. A job that will make use of her higher education – no more tedious vegetable checks!

English

Ever since she had started school, Katarzyna had loved English. Ever since she had her first ever lesson she has adored the language. Even when she was a little girl, only six years old, going to her small, village primary school. It had become her lifelong dream to visit either England or America and to use the English she knew to communicate there and to explore those strange countries.

It was funny, really. Her parents often used English as a punishment for her. For example, they used to make her or her brothers learn more English vocabulary if they were naughty.

Her brothers resented this and always moaned, but it never worked for Katarzyna because she loved English. Sometimes she would get into trouble on purpose just so that she could have time to learn more English! She saw this as a pleasure, not a punishment!

After primary, Katarzyna went to high school in a nearby city. When she went to high school, Katarzyna had to live apart from her parents, like in a boarding school. Can you imagine? Having to live in a strange new town, separated from your family when you are only 14?! But Katarzyna didn't mind. She enjoyed being independent and having the extra freedom. For her A-levels, she took English (naturally!) along with Polish and biology, even though she didn't really like Polish. Her high school was run by nuns and it was a girls' school. It was very strict!

Katarzyna really enjoyed school life, so when she had finished her A-levels (and passed them all too!) she continued on to university where she trained to become a doctor. When the final exam came, she was only two marks short of passing – she was so frustrated! Her education thus far had cost a fortune and now she would either have to redo all of her medical training or take a degree in another subject, costing even more money. Sometimes, I think, people in England take our education for granted because we have the chance to go to school and have a free education. The only part we have to pay for is university, and even then you can get student loans to aid you. People probably don't realise that in other countries, it costs a great deal of money to send a child to school – even other countries in Europe. In the end, Katarzyna chose to study biology, hoping she might pass the exam this time!

Choices

Shortly after this, Katarzyna decided to come to England. She found an organisation that sent her here. It was a long and harsh journey, mostly by a small boat. By the time it arrived here, half the passengers were ill. But Katarzyna was still excited; nothing could dampen her spirits, not even the chilling sea spray. Taking that first step in a foreign land – nothing could compare to the joy and wonder she felt, but also the strange mixture of fear and doubt too. Katarzyna had arrived in England; she had accomplished her dream. And she could actually understand what everyone was saying!

Her first job here was awful – checking vegetables, of all things, in a stuffy little factory near Boston. Working a full day, six days a week, was a drastic change to what she had been used to, but it was still an adventure no matter how tedious! At least she got her own housing! Her boss was actually really nice and they became friends instantly. Lots of her other colleagues were really nice to her too and she made friends quickly. They made her feel at home and she was really enjoying herself too. But, as with all things, after a rather unproductive year, the job became so boring and, after much thought, Katarzyna chose to use some of the money she had earned to go home.

Once back in Poland, Katarzyna decided to pick up where she left off with her studies. By now she had acquired enough money to pay for her own tuition and to pay her parents back for some of the other fees, so Katarzyna could support herself. After leaving England she was still torn between staying or going back again – she just couldn't make up her mind!

Eventually, she chose to quit her studies and return to England – AGAIN! Her parents were disappointed and wanted her to stay, but her mind was now made up. She got her old job back and was happy again. Now was the chance for her to make something of herself.

Today

Walking through the snow, Katarzyna gazed around in wonder, contemplating how she ended up here. Hurrying to work through the streets of Grantham to her fantastic job, she thought about her life. It was fantastic! She had lots of great friends, especially at work, and was really enjoying herself. She was earning a fortune compared to what her family had earned in Poland, and she was thrilled to have her own individual life.

Last November, Katarzyna got a promotion. It was the last thing in the world that she would have expected to happen, but it did happen! And to her too! Now working as an interviewer at the Grantham branch of Lloyds TSB, she found everything was falling into place. Everyone enjoyed seeing her, her customers included. She worked mainly with Polish clients who needed her help with translations. Some days, there were people queuing up to see her!!

The last time she was in Poland was at Christmas. Her family were so happy to see her, but she knew that she didn't want to stay. She was pleased with herself and her opportunities in England and did not want to give that life up for anything, and her parents understood that. Work was hectic, but it was fulfilling and her parents would always support her. They saw how much happier her new life made Katarzyna and they wouldn't want to take that away. She was finally living her dream for good.

Helena Cotterill

Prejudgement

It took a long while to strike me but I learned important lessons during my visit, one morning, to St. Luke's School.

I was specifically picked for my strengths in English and was assigned for a couple of days to Lincoln Bishop Grosseteste College, and then the ten of us one day left our rural school of Welton William Farr to interview various students from St. Luke's School who were born outside Britain.

As we were leaving the school in our little blue van, I wondered what my interview partner would be like. I wondered how the school gets managed and about the atmosphere inside. I was not sure if I was going to be welcomed in or looked down upon, made to feel an outcast from their society.

When the van neared the familiar facilities of St. Luke's, I felt slightly anxious. I was going to visit a different school. It would put my school into perspective.

Our van turned 90 degrees to the right and approached a gate of the intimidatingly large but also pleasant building. I thought to myself, if buildings could talk and substitute people's thoughts, feelings and well-being, what would this building say?

The van stopped and the doors slid open. It was only a few steps before we entered the reception and some of us were already judging the school purely based on the architecture and layout of the reception. I knew some of us had prejudiced feelings because of what we have each individually heard about the school. However, rumours are just like Chinese whispers, they morph and change from person to person; so I banished the Chinese whispers from my mind and hoped for the best from the day.

We were guided through the building. The number of winding corridors and the doors leading off them to areas that I will probably never go to astonished me. Our school has around 11, mostly two-storey, square, rather childlike buildings in comparison, equipped with a simplistic corridor on both floors with two rooms leading off each opposite wall, with bridges interconnecting the range of department facilities. St. Luke's definitely had a historical feeling. I felt slightly jealous.

I noticed as we walked through the labyrinth that the children seemed to be more happy and content than we did. I noticed a teacher really giving a large smile and I thought that was a strange sight. I felt more comfortable at the sound of children laughing and playfully teasing each other with no following sounds of a staff member shouting at them for 'acting childish and immature'. Sixth formers were wearing clothes our school would 'not deem acceptable'.

As I entered a room, I noticed several children dotted around. There were no signs that they weren't average British citizens by the way they dressed, looked or sat.

Two friends and me were seated opposite three girls. Two Polish girls and a Lithuanian. I interviewed one of the two Polish girls. I decided later on that 'interview' wasn't the correct word. At first I wasn't so sure of what to say to her. Hello? Tell me about yourself? I felt so rude and pathetic. So I let her ask me questions first, so I didn't feel I came all this way to intrude.

She knew a little about me now. It made a difference. I asked her a couple of questions but I felt rather awkward. I looked at my classmates, scribbling down as fast as they could whilst nodding their heads with approval.

She came from Poland a couple of years ago, moving because her mother wanted to take up a job here. She explained how she and her sister feel well in England and how much better it is for them. She stressed how hard it is to become friends with English pupils here because of the language barrier, but she gets the extra support. Her best two friends are the two sat beside her, a Polish girl and a Lithuanian.

I was curious to know whether there was much cultural difference between her and me. I asked if she was religious. She was lapsed over religion, surely like the majority of us? She wrote some notes for me. She apologised for her spelling but I told her she spelt how it was pronounced which sounded more logical to me. Her hobbies and interests seemed quite common – she liked to party, she liked films, music, shopping with her friends on Saturdays. I persistently attempted to find heartbreak in her life. I wondered how her home was in Poland; she said she lived in a decent house in a town like she does now in England, she says she's left many family members there; however, she hasn't seen them in years. At the time I thought I had to write about her life at 17 – however, I couldn't find anything obvious to cover. Then she mentioned discrimination.

She's confused about why the country has such hatred for the Polish. She was angered at the way the Polish are described as 'stealing all of the jobs' and how people on the streets look at her like she is a rodent. She says her mum works in a factory. She wonders how that is classed as stealing a job. People call her job stealer, yet she is trying hard at school, working for one. She doesn't understand.

I couldn't really find any more information. I wondered how her thoughts were circulating round her head and what they were. The way the people from two different nations are completely divided and find it so difficult to interact, despite being the same creatures and having identical interests. She seemed like a normal girl who had moved from abroad without having a choice. Why do people expect her to have had a terrible life?

She had lived an ordinary Polish life and now she lives a sub-normal English one, only really interacting with people of her nationality but still trying her best to learn our language. But yet the word 'our' is not right. Because she is one of us, but there are very limited ways to describe exactly what I mean. Language itself is brilliant but it limits people. Because of language, she will live a much harder life here – she has limitations purely based on her language. This links to how people judge the Polish – it has become a commonly held view that Polish people steal jobs – even children who do not understand how careers and employment works say this. It just shows how people prejudge things before they see them just as I was expecting that she was leading a bad life just because she was Polish. Some would find that rather insulting. For example, my school's differences and how a lot of schools compete, yet they all have the same purpose: to educate today's children. So why pre-judge other schools and why the silent competition? Like prejudging the Polish, but yet they are English at the same time. It is just a name for where you were born, but she is being bred here now. Surely if we all live on Mother Earth we are all the same – human. If we really want society to work we need to start practising what we preach more and reorganise our priorities, because if people are thinking of objects and status more than people themselves, surely the point of modern-day existence is foiled. Because of her language she might not ever feel as worthy or whole as we do, and that to me is unnatural. It is God's big mistake, if he is here with us, but definitely each and every one of us is part of that mistake as well.

Stephen Foster

Anita Sevilla-Luthada

The weather is a most popular subject of discussion in Britain. I never really understood why. If you meet somebody in the streets in Britain, they tend to say something like 'Beautiful day!' or 'Lovely weather!' even though it may not be lovely weather at all. I find this ironic considering that Britain has some of the worst weather in the world. Did you know, for instance, that it receives roughly 865 mm of rain every year? And that the average wind speed in a year is 14 mph? Perhaps you weren't aware that the average temperature in winter is 4 °C? I hate British weather.

I tried not to think about this as the rush of cold, very British air slammed into me when I stepped off the plane that had sheltered me from sub-zero temperatures for the past two and a half hours. I shivered and slowly made my way down the steps. Nervous yet excited, hundreds of miles away from my family and friends, I stepped onto England like Cortez had stepped onto Aztec territory so many years ago. I had no idea where to go, but the Spanish embassy was my best option. They could help me get a visa, a job and find me a hotel or at least somewhere I could stay for the night. Knowing this, I hurried indoors to collect my luggage and hopefu— (another gust hit me mid thought) – definitely my coat. Why did England have to be so cold? A man barged past me so I decided to follow him, as he probably knew where we needed to go for luggage collection. I broke into a run to get indoors more quickly.

When I made it inside, after a brief and relatively easy check-in, I looked up at the signs to find out where my luggage was but it was all written in English. When I looked back, the man had gone. I was hopelessly lost in a foreign country with nobody I knew and none of my luggage. After I had wandered around aimlessly for about half an hour, a woman approached me.

'Buenos días,' she said.

I was too tired to be stunned at finding someone who spoke my own language, but replied quickly,

'¿Dónde está recogida de equipaje?'

'¿Recogida de equipaje?' she pointed at a corridor to our left.

I was about to ask how she knew I was Spanish when she presented to me my own passport! Realising I must have dropped it foolishly, I gave her my thanks and proceeded down the corridor to luggage collection. A great start to life in a new country – I was just in time. A suitcase just like mine was being lifted off and put onto a trolley, which I can only assume, led to lost property. I called out to the men lifting it and tried to explain, somewhat desperately, that it was mine. Eventually, they understood the 26-year-old Spanish woman rambling at them and gave it to me. The baggage label had been removed; however, other than that, it seemed to be fine.

That afternoon, after having a walk around the airport and finding out where the embassy was for future reference, I purchased a Spanish-to-English phrase book from a strange shop called 'WH Smith' just outside the airport. My need for the book became all the more apparent when I pulled out a five-euro note to pay for it! Certain it had become even colder than before, I found somewhere to get a warm drink, sat down and had a cup of tea whilst reading my new book. My mother had told me that tea is the most popular drink in England. She said that British people drink 165 million cups of tea a day. I can't see why. I hated it. It had a strange taste when it was warm and had milk mixed into it, which stayed in your mouth for ages and left it feeling stale. 'Stick to iced tea,' I thought. I decided to order a coffee instead. I hoped I would have better luck but it was weak and a strange colour, though when I put sugar in it, it didn't taste as creamy. It was more like milk than coffee. I didn't like it at all.

About 45 minutes later, I decided to go to the embassy. Before braving the outside I went to put my coat on, learning already and so as to not have a repeat of this morning. But as I unzipped my suitcase and put my hand in, I had a feeling something was not quite right. And when I pulled out a pair of men's swimming shorts, I knew something was definitely wrong...

George Lord

Mehmet

I saw the clouds break as I awoke after the apparently short four-hour flight over the skies of Europe. I had seen the sky change from the beloved blue of Turkey, as clear as glass, and as blue as the Mediterranean Sea itself, to a dull rolling mass of grey cloud, which shrouded the feeble light and warmth of the British sun.

It was my first time on a plane, and it had been an alien occurrence. I was going beyond anywhere I had been before, to a new country, a new environment and to new experiences. Doubts still lingered over my abrupt decision to leave my homeland, my life and my family. It had been a hard choice, but it was too late to change the result now. There was no going back.

I had felt the subtle movement of the plane as it tilted down, making minute amendments as it prepared for landing. The landing gear extended underneath my feet, vibrating the bodywork of the plane, as the seatbelt sign blinked on, confirming my theory that we were soon to land. Another confirmation as the pilot announced, 'Ladies and gentlemen, we are preparing to land: please put on your seatbelt and do not remove it until you are instructed to by an air steward and the plane has safely landed…'

Left, right, up and down. Everywhere was different. Everything had changed. New surroundings, a new life, a fresh start. I had arrived. It was around two o'clock in the morning, since I had caught a late flight, wanting to begin my new life as quickly as possible.

It was a dull place. The dark grey floor, the high oppressive ceiling, the hustle of passengers oozing through passport control. It was not so much a queue as a mass of people slowly creeping through the understaffed tills, into what is called 'Manchester Airport'.

Security was everywhere, I was scared that I might be apprehended and sent back to Turkey. They watched me, crossing the short space into the back of the 'queue', observing the fact that many eyes were on me, both human and the mechanical eye of the security cameras.

I was still there half an hour later. The flight had backlogged into another, and I was impatient. I wanted to get through, I wanted to reboot my life, and start again afresh. An old, solitary woman approached from behind me, attempting to push through the line, through passport control. I could smell the cheap, musky fragrance of market perfume from her old patched clothes as I was pressed into her closer presence by the waiting people behind me. I could also detect a heavy undertone of alcohol and I remember thinking, as I recoiled, slightly nauseated and profoundly disgusted, that no amount of tacky perfume could ever cover that smell.

After waiting for another hour, being constantly shunted to the side, and being regarded with suspicion, I finally reached the control desk, where a young woman in an untidy blue and white uniform stood wearing a false smile. 'Could I see your passport please?' she said, in a strong Mancunian accent which I found difficult to understand, and I stood uncomfortably, awkwardly, waiting for her to repeat, as I tried to gain the courage to ask her what she meant.

An impatient man of advancing girth and retreating hairline was standing behind me, annoyed at the wait and the time it was taking him to get through the gate, so he shouted in my ear, 'Show her your bloody passport, we don't all have forever,' and under his breath, he remarked, 'Bloody foreigners'. I would have responded but, eager to be away, I showed the woman my passport and moved on.

Minutes later, I stood at a junction, confused. There were signs everywhere. People everywhere.

I followed everyone else and found my way past the baggage section, into the main lobby. The size… it was huge. Windows towering high above the door, letting in a true British autumn – murky, overcast sky, with rain drizzling down the windows. The polished floor was beating with staccato ring of footsteps. Families and couples alike, walking, running, hustling, bustling around, and slowly working their way through the intimidating, revolving, polished metal doors.

I stood. Still. Silent. Shock and excitement. Realisation. Realisation that I had arrived. My destination: Manchester, England, a new home.

My new home…

Daniel Walker

Being Free

Walking up the driveway I was becoming apprehensive. I knew nothing about this man. I had only found out where he came from a few weeks previously. Would he have an interesting story to tell? Not everyone can have tragic lives or interesting events happen to them. His house was warm and inviting and I sat around the dining room table with Mike, his wife, and my Mum. And so I began the interview. Mike sat tall in his chair, wearing a pale blue shirt that matched his eyes. His hair was in disarray, turning grey with a few tints of hazel throughout.

Mike was born in Zimbabwe. I knew little of this country other than that it was in Africa. I had heard about the conflict occurring there in passing but it seemed a million miles away from my life here; not my problem. Now Mike was recounting his story first-hand and it was suddenly very real and very unexpected. His grandfather originally moved to Zimbabwe, then known as Rhodesia, and was a respected worker helping to manage the establishment of the railway network in the north of the country. His son, Mike's father, was soon to follow in his footsteps and in later life he received the MBE from the queen for his contribution. Mike was born in Salisbury in 1955 and spent much of the earlier part of his life moving around the country, due to his father's job, before settling in Bulawayo where he was to live until he was 15 years old.

Mike seemed very reserved as he began to tell his story. He was very polite, giving me facts but not much else. His underlying tone, however, was very different. It is obvious that he is fiercely proud of his country and his home. He didn't have a bad word to say about either.

One of Mike's earliest memories was when, at the age of six, he was given his first bicycle. This was soon to become a big part of his life and he would ride his bike around the city. Sometimes during the summer he would venture into the countryside with his friends to go camping, something I myself despise with a passion.

The idyllic countryside was a reminder of what a beautiful country he was privileged to live in. They would cycle down to Matobo, or on occasions to a place called Melini where there was a dam. They rode along the scorched paths, baked and cracked by the sun, worn down by the vehicles passing, through the years, and, looking back, this was probably the most innocent time of his life. What he didn't know was the underlying tension arising in the country around him.

Mike had a decent upbringing. His family were neither very poor nor very rich, yet Mike was never deprived of anything in his childhood. His family would holiday in South Africa by the beach, the sands famous for their brilliant white colour and the sea aquamarine blue. However, Mike's most prominent memory of his early years was being free. You could go wherever you wanted and do whatever you wanted without any kind of persecution. As far as blacks were concerned there was some segregation, but Mike saw it more as a peasantry side of the population and it was not very evident in his life. This seems almost alien in the society I live in today. Mothers are scared to let their children leave the house and everyone is always judging one another. Everyone seems so desperate to conform to the stereotype of the 'perfect' person that it makes Mike's world seem idyllic in comparison.

Mike's two elder sisters went to the convent school, which meant Mike had to attend a Christian Brothers' School that was a privately run institution. He had a good education but his schooling was strict and rules were toughly enforced. Perhaps a feeling of déjà vu, it is strange to see how little schooling changes across the countries and decades. School uniform had to be worn perfectly, hair had to be the right length and the boys had to wear their blazers even in the summer. There were hair checks every two weeks and if their hair was even a little bit too long they were given detention. When he was 15 Mike and his family moved to Salisbury and he finished his education at Churchill School, named after the British Prime Minister. Mike stressed that while his schooling was very strict, it was extremely good and the discipline stood him in good stead for later life.

There is a faint smile on his lips all the while he is telling me this. It is obviously a fond memory. Mike's early life seems so much simpler than mine but, of course, I have not heard the entire story. It seems like everything was orderly. He went to school to get a good education; he spent his spare time having fun. In our modern day world there is much more pressure: to be clever, pretty and popular – a stereotype enforced by TV and film.

Mike's two sisters both went to university in South Africa but by the time it was Mike's turn his family could not quite afford to send him as well. Instead, he took a three-year teaching course at the Bulawayo Teacher's College, part of the University of Rhodesia, where he graduated with a Diploma.

For many years Mike was a member of the college choir, which was very well regarded and, in his final few weeks at college, he travelled with them on a tour of England performing in schools and churches around the south of the country. This was the first time Mike was to come to England and was a completely new experience for all the boys, as the culture was so different and most of them had never been outside of their own country. It was a fabulous trip and they all enjoyed it hugely. Within a month of returning to Rhodesia, Mike was conscripted into the army.

Troubled Times

In order to understand the tensions and troubles within the country, it is necessary to look into its recent history. Known previously as Rhodesia, it was a British colony ruled by a white elite class who provided the country with an excellent infrastructure and education system. By making use of the skills of the British and taking advantage of the cheap black labour, the country thrived economically. Being rich in minerals and having very fertile lands, it was known as the breadbasket of Africa. In the late sixties the British Government started granting independence to its African colonies such as Zambia and Malawi, but would not do so for Rhodesia. The major stumbling block was the fact that all wealth was in the hands of the whites, who also governed the country. The white Rhodesians wanted their enviable lifestyle to continue but the world was changing and full democracy could be the only acceptable solution for the UK. Frustrated by the situation, Rhodesia declared independence in 1965.

The situation was ripe for the emergence of a leader who could topple the all-white Government and champion the cause of the majority black population. That leader was Robert Mugabe. Due to his dictatorship, the country soon fell into decline and today, cholera is rife and life expectancy is at an all-time low.

There followed many years of difficulty and unrest for Rhodesia. A large army was needed to fight a bush war along the borders against local guerrillas whose aim was to destabilise the government. Many Western countries had also imposed trading sanctions.

Rhodesia finally lost the battle, and in 1979 a transition began which led to the election in 1980 of Robert Mugabe and the country being renamed Zimbabwe.

Corruption and inefficiency soon became widespread and this once prosperous country fell into a steady decline. Lands were seized from whites, and many of the educated classes left with no one to replace the skills and knowledge that went with them. The country is now a shambles, with most people without work or a means to exist at anything more than the most basic level; people are starving and the country suffers from hyperinflation.

Now Mike's hands are clasped on the table and the horrors of what he has been through are all too apparent. The trials and troubles of his country had a major impact upon Mike's life. During the bush war years, all young men had to do an initial one year of training and service in the army and then would subsequently spend six weeks in and six weeks out. In some respects Mike was lucky; because of his chosen profession as a teacher he was able to lead a more orderly life, being called up to serve a term every now and again. Setting aside the seriousness of the situation, Mike enjoyed the discipline and physical demands of his national service. This displays a recurring theme in Mike's life where order and decency are an important part of how he lives.

Mike underplays his time in the army where he served as an

officer. It was clearly a very dangerous situation and sadly friends and acquaintances were not as lucky as Mike. Today in the media we constantly see the tragedy that war creates and the devastation brought to the families involved.

In-between his terms of service in the army, Mike was progressing quickly in his teaching career, moving swiftly from teacher, to superintendent, deputy and then headmaster. During his time as deputy in Hartley, another life-changing event occurred. He met Christine, a beautiful, newly qualified, young teacher who would eventually become his wife. In this period, life couldn't have been much better – he and Christine enjoyed a beautiful house, with lovely grounds and a pool. He was paid well and played golf every week; free time was spent socialising at barbecues, enjoying the constant blue skies and blissful surroundings. A huge advantage of being a teacher at this time in Rhodesia was the assurance of high-quality housing that came with the job. They were delighted when they became a family with the arrival of first a baby girl and then a baby boy.

Whilst the wider picture was becoming increasingly disturbing, in general day-to-day life remained largely untouched; however, the first seeds of doubt were beginning to form in Mike and Christine's minds and they just hoped that they were wrong.

I can empathise with how Mike and Christine must have been beginning to feel right now. This perfect country in which they have grown up is beginning to fall apart, resulting in a feeling of hopelessness, just not knowing where their future lies. The absolute powerlessness of the population to overrule the government that is destroying everything generations of families have worked for, is devastating.

Leaving the Country

By 1997 the Zimbabwean economy was in a steep decline. Intimidation and violence were not uncommon and many of the educated population were leaving. The financial state of the country was in a mess. There were shortages of all foodstuffs and fuels. Mike and Christine were beginning to lose students and so had concerns for job security. In addition they were feeling the effects of inflation and their comfortable lifestyle was being eroded. They had major concerns about funding their children's education and they believed they would eventually leave the country anyway. They made the hugely difficult decision to leave as a family rather than to risk separation from their children in later years.

Mike and Christine were not the only ones making tough decisions. Mike's two sisters were already living in South Africa. However, Christine's parents were in a more desperate situation. As a retired bank manager, her father had looked forward to a comfortable and happy retirement but instead had to endure the prospect of emigrating just in order to pay for his diabetes medication.

Mike came over on his own in 2001 to make some money. He originally went fruit picking for a month in Kent and that made enough money for him to get back to Zimbabwe. This was a huge contrast with being a teacher and huge step down from the position of power he had had and the respect he had back home.

He came again on his own in February and joined a computer firm in London. That gave him enough money to bring his family over and for the first time they were all here. He tried teaching but the system was so different from his own back home. The discipline he had always integrated into his method of teaching didn't fit this much more modern schooling system and he did not feel he could continue working in that field. Also, he was living off an unqualified teacher's salary because the government would not accept his diploma. This new country was completely foreign to him: the culture, the people and his position in life. He had previously been well respected and well liked among his peers and now he had to struggle to find where his place was in this new order of things.

He joined an ink production company in Bottesford and helped perfect that for two years before moving on to work as a warehouse manager for a company making beanbag furniture. He now works as a lorry driver, because he can do it any time and he still has an old bus driving licence from Rhodesia. All he had to do was renew his lorry driver's licence. The job pays almost as much as a teacher's salary and Mike says it keeps him sane.

Life in England is very different from life in Rhodesia. Back there his house was provided with the job and he had acres of land. The country was very open and bright, whereas here it is becoming overcrowded and has a cool climate. However, he does not regret leaving. The country he left has now turned into one of poverty, corruption and violence. Here he has a safe and secure way of life and he can put food on the table. He can educate his two children, and their opportunities are endless.

It is obvious that Mike and Christine are very proud of the country of their birth, and rightly so. The country was very strong and could have become very successful, but by the time Mugabe came to power they had to leave. While the rest of their family moved to South Africa they stayed, believing – perhaps foolishly – that blacks and whites could work together in the country, but it was not to be. There will always be questions of 'what if?' and I am sure Mike and Christine hope for the day when they can return to their country and experience again the hope and freedom with which they grew up.

Alexandra Slipper

Further Reading

If you are interested in the themes covered in this book you may want to explore them further by reading some of the following books:

The Arrival by Shaun Tan
(Hodder, ISBN 9780340969939)
– a surreal account of the experience of immigration.

The Island by Armin Greder
(Allen and Unwin, ISBN 9781741752663)
– a very powerful picture book.

The Complete Maus by Art Spiegelman
(Penguin, ISBN 0141014083)
– a graphic novel telling the story of the author's father's escape from
Nazi- occupied Poland.

Persepolis by Marjane Satrapi
(Vintage, ISBN 9780099523994)
– a graphic novel about growing up in Iran.

What Is She Doing Here? by Kate Clanchy
(Picador, ISBN 9780330443821)
– the biography of a Kosovan refugee that inspired this project.

The Road Home by Rose Tremain
(Vintage, ISBN-10: 0099478463)
– the story of a middle-aged Polish worker who moves to London.

Boy Overboard by Morris Gleitzman
(Puffin, ISBN-10: 014131625X)
– the story of a family who leave Afghanistan to start a new life in Australia.

Girl Underground by Morris Gleitzman
(Puffin, ISBN-10: 0141319003)
– the story of some Australian children who take matters into their own hands to
help others locked in a detention centre.